*The Family
and
the Fellowship*

Also by Ralph Martin:

MARK: EVANGELIST AND THEOLOGIAN
COLOSSIANS: THE CHURCH'S LORD AND THE CHRISTIAN'S
LIBERTY
NEW TESTAMENT FOUNDATIONS
    VOL. 1 THE FOUR GOSPELS
    VOL. 2 ACTS—REVELATION

THE FAMILY
AND
THE FELLOWSHIP:
New Testament Images of the Church

by
RALPH P. MARTIN

Professor of New Testament,
Fuller Theological Seminary,
Pasadena, California

Grand Rapids
WILLIAM B. EERDMANS PUBLISHING COMPANY

Copyright © Ralph P. Martin 1979.

First published 1979 by The Paternoster Press Ltd., England.

First American edition published 1980 through special arrangement with Paternoster by Wm. B. Eerdmans Publishing Co., 255 Jefferson Ave. S. E., Grand Rapids, Mich. 49503.

Library of Congress Cataloging in Publication Data

Martin, Ralph P
    The family and the fellowship

    Includes index.
    1.   Church — Biblical teaching.   2.   Bible.   N.T. —
Criticism, interpretation, etc.   I.   Title.
BS2545.C5M33   1980   262'.7   80-127
ISBN 0-8028-1829-3

This book
is for
Sarah Elizabeth
and
Michelle Lynne
in the prayerful hope
that the church as they
will know it may be
worthier of its name
than the church today

Contents

Abbreviations

ET	English translation
Moffatt	James Moffatt, *A New Translation of the Bible*, 1936
NEB	New English Bible, 1970
RSV	Revised Standard Version, 1952
TDNT	*Theological Dictionary of the New Testament*, vols. 1–9, edd. G. Kittel and G. Friedrich, ET by G. W. Bromiley, 1964–74

Preface

The aim of this little book ought to be confessed at the outset. Admittedly there are several useful books on the nature and life of the Christian church on the market today. Why then add yet another title?

The author's conviction is that many Christians today need to see the necessary place of the church in God's design and to take a positive attitude to it. Each chapter, then, may well lead to an enhanced appreciation of what church life can mean in both descriptive and practical (mainly in chapter 9) terms.

The intention of the writer has been to produce a simply composed yet fairly comprehensive summary of what the New Testament has to say about selected themes of the church and its role in the believer's life. Some sentences may well need a qualifying footnote to direct attention to alternative views, but I have tried to resist that particular temptation. A few bibliographical details are however added. Scripture quotations are taken from the *Good News Bible*, usually from the 1976 edition but occasionally from the 1966 New Testament version.

This volume is taking final shape not a half-mile from the traditional sites on Mount Zion in Jerusalem where Pentecost occurred and the first Christian church met in the upper room of the Last Supper and the post-resurrection gatherings (Acts 1:13). There will always be a difference of opinion about the scene of the Cenacle and the presence of early Christians on Mount Zion, near the so-called Gate of the Essenes. But these disputable matters apart, it is certainly an inspiring task to be writing these chapters and, with a moment's pause, to look across the Hinnom valley and with a short walk, to re-visit the Mount of Olives and to look across the Kidron to places which Jesus and the first apostles once knew so well. A term's sabbatical leave at the Institute of Holy Land Studies has made the composing of this book in these circumstances a memorable experience.

Ralph P. Martin

Jerusalem
November 1978

1
The Church: The Birth of an Idea

Our Human Life: Personal and Corporate

In this opening section we take a look at the concept of the church and ask where the idea came from. Let us begin with ourselves, since this is a reality of which we are all immediately aware. There is no denying, at least for most people who are unconcerned with the philosophical questions, that we are living at this present moment in time and that we enjoy separate and distinctive identities.

By our share in the human family we are *both* inescapably personal *and* inevitably social. Our humanness is a fact of experience, and it enables us to affirm both our individual identity and our membership in the larger unit of society around us. In a self-reflective mood I am aware that I am what I am, and there is no one like me. Everyone is unique, however much we may share common physical features and possess similar traits of temperament that govern predictable patterns of behaviour. This consciousness of personal identity involves an inescapable responsibility which, for the Christian, lays upon him or her a claim to heed and respond to the will of God who has loved us into life and calls each person to fellowship with himself. The time-honoured word to describe both our responsibility and our 'responsability,' as Emil Brunner was fond of saying[1] (so uniting our opportunity to hear God's voice and our need to answer its call), is *conversion*. The term has meaning only as it underscores the requirement that each person is answerable to God as an individual. John Bunyan put it in forceful English: 'Every tub must stand on its own bottom.' And equally the response of commitment that is made to God's call is possible only as each one answers with his own affirmation. H. R. Mackintosh wrote finely of this essential requirement:

> Faith, for the mind of the New Testament, is the act in which the fundamentally right relation to God is actualised. Personal trust makes the trusting man righteous in God's sight; it is the attitude – in fact, the only attitude – which contents the Father's heart.[2]

So becoming and being a Christian is a personal, 'privatized' affair; no one can do it for us. It is as solitary and individual as birth and death. Indeed the terminal metaphors of 'being born' and 'having to die' are used in the Bible in exactly this way as they describe impressively the inescapable, personal nature of the Christian life as a new birth and a dying to self (John 3; 1 Peter 1:23, 2:2; Rom. 6:1–11; Col. 3:5–11).

But this emphasis needs some corrective adjustment. For it is equally the case that our full experience of being human is possible only in a community of other people, and we attain the richness of our life only as we enjoy it in society. The philosopher Gabriel Marcel has put it in an epigram: 'to exist is to co-exist' (*esse est co-esse*). Scripture also recognizes this truth in the creation story. 'God created human beings, making them to be like himself. He created them male and female' (Gen. 1:27).

Social psychology is built on the same principle, and it is a recognized commonplace that human behaviour cannot be understood if we foolishly overlook the inherited tendencies, instinctual drives, and latent pressures as well as the more obvious forces that shape our response to the society in which we are born and where we live out our days. John S. Whale uses a couple of well-known examples from literature.[3] Robinson Crusoe was able to survive on his desert island because he brought with him the memory of 'life-together' with other fellowmen and women before he met man Friday. On the other hand, Tarzan of the apes is a fiction because we are asked to think of him as human *before* he met Jane; and that awareness of being human could only have been his by his associating with other human beings.

The New Testament is just as insistent that conversion is the gateway leading to inclusion within a wider fellowship. The verses that come most readily to mind are clear:

> For Christ is like a single body, which has many parts; it is still one body, even though it is made up of different parts. . . . All of you, then, are Christ's body, and each one is a part of it.
>
> (1 Corinthians 12:12, 27)

> None of us lives for himself only, none of us dies for himself only.
>
> (Romans 14:7)

> We are all members together in the body of Christ.
>
> (Ephesians 4:25)

These statements add up to enforce the conclusion that the new life in Christ, admittedly personal, requires a social context for its maintenance and maturity. The Christian life is possible – in all but extraordinary circumstances – only within a network of inter-personal relationships that both lay their claims upon us and invite us to contribute our best. In a word, 'being a Christian' includes *both* the individual response each must make to the offer and demand of the good news that came with Jesus Christ *and* the entry into a new sphere of social patterns, a community of our fellow believers without whom we fail to achieve our full stature as men and women 'in Christ' (Eph. 4:13). To reach that conclusion is to tread on the threshold of the idea of the church.

Some Consequences

So we need the church. The 'church' in this setting is the company of our fellow Christian believers with whom God has been pleased to join us in the act of incorporating us into the body of Christ (1 Cor. 12:12,13) and without whom each of us fails to attain the full stature of Christian maturity (Eph. 4:13–16). Two supporting reasons for this statement follow:

a. Christian experience is always 'ecclesiastical' experience. Evangelical Protestantism is likely to hiccup at that bald remark, but a moment's reflection will show that it is undoubtedly the case that we depend on others both for our knowledge of Christ and our growth into him. It is a matter of plain fact that the Christian message has reached us through other people. We may think of parents, friends, Sunday school teachers, ministers and evangelists, and writers of literature. Their influence, example and words have proved a turning point in our lives. But even if it were none of these influences that directly led to conversion, it still remains true that no one ever was persuaded and won without a knowledge of elementary biblical truth, called 'the message about Christ' (Rom. 10:17). Once this point is conceded, Professor Lampe's corollary follows: 'Even those Christians who have been brought to conversion through their solitary reading of the Bible have in fact derived their faith from other people – the biblical authors.'[4]

Failure to grasp this sense of the indebtedness we owe to others is often at the root of much dissatisfaction with the church. Unwittingly those who profess that they have no need of the church range themselves with the unthinking Corinthians who set up a gnostic-like conventicle and received the well-merited rebuke of Paul (1 Cor. 14:36) who had just reminded them of their common life in the body of Christ that no schism should tear apart (1 Cor. 12:14–27).

b. The Christianity then that meets us in the pages of the New Testament and that shows itself as a living force across the long haul of history implies churchmanship. Reformers who are often regarded as exponents of unremitting evangelicalism with its stress on the importance of personal faith have placed equal emphasis on the corporate nature of that faith. Sometimes the language about the visible church is hardly congenial to the thinking and preaching of their popularizers; but the Reformed and evangelical statements of faith are clear, even if they do not exactly use the metaphors of Calvin:

Let us learn from her single title of Mother how useful,

indeed how necessary the knowledge of her is. Since there is no other means of entering into life unless she conceives us in the womb and give us birth. . . . Moreover, beyond the pale of the Church no forgiveness of sins, no salvation can be hoped for. . . . It follows that revolt from the Church is denial of God and Christ.[5]

A clear case of the interfacing of personal response and the call to churchmanship may sum it up. If ever there was an individual who could justifiably regard himself as a 'special' convert, an object of divine choice and singular grace par excellence and so one who hardly needed the companionship and help of lesser mortals, it was Saul of Tarsus. He was miraculously converted by a personal encounter with the living Lord who spoke his name (Acts 9:4,5) and seized him for his own service (Phil. 3:12; Gal. 1:15,16; compare Acts 26:16–18). The story of Paul's conversion to his new life does not end there. Indeed, it is not fully told without the assistance of Ananias (Acts 9:6, 10–19, 22:12–16) and Barnabas (Acts 9:26–28). Nor is it a complete record that fails to include Paul's desire to associate with the Christians at Damascus (Acts 9:19–22) and later at Jerusalem (Acts 9:26). The gates of the new experience of life-in-Christ that opened so marvellously on the Damascus highway swung open also to beckon him to the fellowship of men and women 'in Christ' before him (Rom. 16:7). Right from his first days when he heard Ananias' voice, 'Brother Saul' (Acts 9:17), he came to look on the face of his fellow believers as mirroring the image of the glorious Christ (2 Cor. 8:23) and as his brothers and sisters in him (1 Cor. 8:11–13).

Jesus and the Church

One of the most complex problems of current New Testament study is to define precisely the relationship of Jesus to what became known as 'the church.' We may freely concede that all that developed into an organized, structured and institutional entity known as 'the church' in the later centuries may well have been alien to his mind. That is not the point. The issue is whether Jesus in any way envisaged a continuance of that nuclear society known as 'the disciples' which he gathered around him in Galilee and led to Jerusalem for the last, fateful encounter with his enemies. To those men, called by the technical expression the 'Twelve' – even when their number is in doubt as it is at 1 Corinthians 15:5 – he gave the promise of 'au revoir' (Mark 14:25,28) as he bade them 'adieu' just before his passion and death. The pledge of a renewal of fellowship lies deeply embedded in the gospel tradition; the question is whether Jesus thought that the reunion would be in a perfected kingdom of God (as evidently Mark 9:1, 14:25 imply) or a resumption of relations with his disciples after death (as Mark 16:7 most naturally reads). The scholarly debate has continued, ever since Albert Schweitzer posed the problem[6] in its sharp formulation and concluded that the former alternative must be accepted since Jesus' prediction of an end of the age failed to materialize. He died in abject despair with no supernatural intervention to save him.

But we are not driven to that conclusion. More likely is the second alternative, as critics of Schweitzer and his followers have shown. This means that Jesus, for all his anticipation of the crisis that he faced in Jerusalem, still hoped for and planned a renewal of links with the 'Twelve.' Thereafter he would commission them to be his agents in the world, and it was in anticipation of their place in the new age that he sat down at the last supper meal (Luke 22:14–30) and bequeathed to them the privilege and duty of being founder members of the new Israel. The post-resurrection appearances placed the seal of his victory on these promises and articulated what their place in the new Israel was to be. It was a vocation spelled out in terms of mission, witness, and a continuance of his messianic ministry.

We should probably read the celebrated scenario of Matthew 16:13–20 in the light of the Easter experience, though a persuasive case has been offered for treating it as a preview of what the post-resurrection commissioning more fully clarified. The strongest factor is the proposal to read 'I will build my church' as a declaration of intent that says more of Jesus' own mission as an eschatological figure, charged with introducing the new era of God's salvation than of 'the church' as an institutional entity. 'My church' in this reference as well as 'the church' in Matthew 18:15–20 are double allusions to the 'people of God' whom Jesus came to call as a direct result of his Galilean ministry, even if those scholars are correct who see in these verses a reformulation of the Lord's mind for the church in a later period when the congregations became organized and were faced with issues and problems that had not arisen during the lifetime of the Galilean disciples and the earthly Jesus.[7] A case in point is Matthew 18:19,20 which casts the promise of the risen Lord on to a canvas of scattered Christian communites and isolated groups of believers in the later church.

The intention of Jesus to gather a new people of God arose directly out of his prior commitment to that new age that brought him on to the stage of history. His opening words announced the manifesto: 'The appointed time has come to its fulfilment; the rule of God is touching human lives. Turn back to God, and put your trust in the good news' (Mark 1:15). If there is one characteristic slogan that Jesus' ministry in word and deed (Luke 11:20) embodied it is this: the kingdom of God, his rule over the world visibly known and enjoyed, is here. Prepare for it and live by it.

If this conviction of the new age already dawning, with its offer and its demand, is what Jesus' ministry was all about, we can draw out some consequences for the men and women to whom this call was first addressed. The lines of proof can be swiftly established:

a. The kingdom of God as Jesus announced it is likened to a tree whose branches reach out to provide shelter and lodging for 'the birds of the air' (Mark 4:30–32). His hearers would link this picture with the prophets' words about God's plan to call nations and peoples into his realm (Ezek. 17:23, 31:6; Dan. 4:11,12,21).[8] That prophetic dream Jesus boldly claimed as a present reality. And in the strength of his conviction he reached out to call those whom the religious leaders rejected as outcasts and sinners (Mark 2:15–17; Luke 15:1,2; Luke 7:34,35). The most obvious feature of Jesus' Galilean ministry is seen just here: he extended in God's name a personal call to the 'non-religious,' the Jews who had made themselves as Gentiles by reason of their failure to aspire to the heights of a punctilious observance of rabbinic religion, and he openly associated with them. He invited them to enter God's kingdom of grace and receive it as a free gift; and as they responded they were becoming God's people of the new age, his 'church.'

b. The imagery of sheep and shepherd is different and the picture of God's care for individuals is more sharply focused in parables such as those in Luke 15, but it is the same basic idea as we considered a moment ago. The individuals are sought and found, such as Zaccheus (Luke 19:1–10) but the new life that awaits them is societal, involving fresh obligations as well as unheard-of privileges. Zaccheus is a 'son of Abraham,' a member of the new Israel. The shepherd is busy searching out his wandering sheep, unlike the faithless 'shepherds of Israel' (Ezek. 34) who reappear in the religious leaders of Jesus' day. Yet the sheep, now reclaimed and secure in the assurance of the shepherd's care (John 10:11, 14–16), are part of his 'flock' which is none other than the 'flock of God' who inherit the kingdom (Luke 12:32).

c. The summons to Zaccheus was authorized by 'the Son of man' (Luke 19:10). Once more we touch bedrock in the assertion that no self-designation is more fundamental to Jesus' ministry than this description. Whether it is a round-about way of Jesus' announcing himself with a cipher for 'I' or a titular claim which asserted his authority as prophetic or messianic, there is little doubt it goes back to Daniel 7:13. There 'the Son of man' is escorted to the heavenly throne and exalted. But the vision is enlarged in the accompanying commentary, and the reader learns that this elevation is one that includes the receiving a kingdom and the rulership over 'all people, nations, and languages' who serve him as 'the saints of the Most High' who receive and possess the kingdom (Dan. 7:14,18,22,27). Clearly when Jesus claimed to be 'Son of man' it was more than a vocation involving only himself; it entailed the destiny of a people associated with him both in suffering and triumph, his 'church.'

d. Those people were concentrated in the men whom Jesus called to be with him (Mark 3:13,14). Acting in the manner of Isaiah the prophet (Isa. 8:16–18), he gathered twelve followers to whom he gave special responsibility and special training. For they, twelve in number as representing the twelve sons of Jacob and the tribes of Israel, were to be the nucleus of the Israel of the new covenant. The high point of their training and experience was to come as they sat down at a Passover meal and were invited to enter into covenantal relations with their host (Luke 22:29,30). To them the kingdom would be entrusted as they were faithful to the task Jesus laid upon them. Acting out the terms of the new covenant, ratified by his sacrifice and triumph, they would be his agents to extend and enlarge his ministry throughout the world. For this he had summoned, trained, and commissioned them; and to them he promised the Spirit as their abiding gift. All these experiences served to enforce their sense of being God's people in embryo, yet destined to grow and develop to become the body of Christ in the world, as Paul was later to frame this initial understanding. But the turning point was revealed when, having glimpsed who Jesus was, God's messiah (Mark 8:29), they had to learn that he was God's agent *to do his will in his way.*[9] The Son of man must suffer before he is exalted. And they are called to share both his humiliation and his victory.

At the supper table they sit down to see dramatized in symbolic fashion what price God's messiah will have to pay as the suffering one and how vindication comes only as he – and they – are faithful to the end. They sit down as the church-in-miniature; and in a brief moment they glimpse what Jesus has come to be and to do.

2
The Church at Pentecost

Where It All Began

The narrative in Acts chapter two is the place where the church reads its birth story. Its genealogy is traced back to a momentous occasion when, during the Jewish festival of Weeks, 'seven weeks' following Passover in the year Jesus died and rose again, a new chapter in world history was written and the course of human life was set in a fresh direction. The 'turning point of the ages,' established by the events of Jesus' death, and his resurrection and exaltation, is played out in the drama of changed lives and the appearing of a new society. The link-term that unites the ascension of Jesus to the Father's presence and the emergence of 'the church' as a historical reality is *the coming of the Holy Spirit*. Peter explains this in a key sentence of the first Christian sermon:

> He has been raised to the right side of God and received from him the Holy Spirit, as his Father had promised; and what you now see and hear is his gift that he has poured out on us.
>
> (Acts 2:33)

Exactly when the church began is not clearly known. It could be argued that 'the people of God' have existed in the world since Abraham's call and response (Gen. 12:1-3, 15:5), and we are bidden recall our origins in Isaiah 51:2: 'Think of your ancestor, Abraham . . . [and] I blessed him and gave him children; I made his descendants numerous.' Paul finds no incongruity in describing the patriarch as 'our forefather'

22

(Rom. 4:1, RSV), and states that Gentiles like the Galatians are now made 'children of Abraham' by faith in Israel's messiah (Gal. 3:6–14).

The people of God who were led into the wilderness as they journeyed from Egypt to the land promised to Abraham and his family are called by the precise title 'the church' (Acts 7:38), since they were the assembled company whom God rescued and made his own people by election and the covenant.

The followers of Jesus received the promise of a 'new covenant' announced by Jeremiah (31:31–34) to replace the Sinai covenant to which the Jews were not faithful (Heb. 8:8–13). The new start that was made in Jesus' ministry saw the rebirth of the church as God's people. So it could equally be said that the 'church' began with a new, deeper meaning as Jesus' call, 'Follow me', was heard and responded to; or that it was in the hour of divine disclosure and human perception when at Caesarea Philippi Peter announced, 'You are the messiah' that the church was reborn. But it is more likely that no 'church' in the strict sense of that term existed until the events of salvation history had been enacted. We must give full weight to the coming of the new age, inaugurated at messiah's sacrifice and vindication; and while it is true that the Twelve sat down in the upper room as the 'church-in-embryo,' the people of God in the full sense of that term came to birth only after the Easter triumph. Whatever else the church is called to be it is essentially 'the community of the risen Lord'; and in the final sense it can only be said to exist on the near side of what happened at Calvary and on the third day later. All else was preparatory and in anticipation; once Jesus emerged as the Lord of Easter and the dispenser of the Spirit the church was ready to be born.[1] The days of Pentecost were the final gestation period; and the day that marked the descent of the Spirit constituted the church's *dies natalis*, its birthday, as Augustine perceived.

Birthday joys are an occasion of celebration; and it is not out of place to remark on the note of joy that pervades the narrative in Acts (2:28,46). A historical allusion in a later period drives home the point. An early English chronicler wrote of the crowning of king Edgar in Bath Abbey in AD 973:

> Much bliss was there by all enjoyed
> On that happy day named Pentecost
> By men below.

What Happened at Pentecost?[2]

The phenomena associated with the Spirit's coming are all mysterious. Luke's cautiously framed language[3] shows that he is aware of this. There was a noise which sounded like the blowing of a strong wind. What looked like tongues of fire were distributed over the heads of the assembled men and women, 120 in number. There was communication as they opened their mouths to give utterance to 'the great things that God has done' (Acts 2:11); and they all spoke so unitedly and harmoniously that language barriers were crossed. There was immediate rapport between speaker and hearer, even though the speakers were 'all Galileans' (2:7), known for their accent as Peter's speech had earlier identified him in the high priest's courtyard and although the auditors were drawn from all points and countries of the Jewish dispersion around the Mediterranean world.

Luke's manner of writing suggests that we should relate the historical events to their symbolic meaning. 'Wind' is preparing us to hear about God's 'wind,' the spirit, since both Hebrew and Greek have but one word to define what is meant by both ideas (see John 3:8 for a good illustration of this). 'Fire' is a clear picture word for the divine presence, visible and alive as in the story of Exodus 19:16–18, 24:17. 'Tongues' suggest instant, unmediated communication that reversed the judgment of the Tower of Babel (Gen. 11:1–9) when 'the Lord mixed up the language of all the people; and from there he scattered them all over the earth' (11:9). 'They did not understand one another's speech' (11:7 RSV) was a sad consequence of human arrogance and *hybris* at Babel. At Pentecost that judgment is upturned, and it is possible for God's mighty acts in Jesus to be rehearsed and celebrated with no language impediment. The *glossolalia* sounds as if there were a divine shortcut to the Berlitz school;[4] yet at a deeper level it was not so much the fact of immediate comprehension that arrested the hearers' attention. What evoked their wonder and led to some natural suspicion of intoxication (v. 12) was *what these people said*. They were claiming to be entering across the threshold of a new world. They were announcing a new calendar, saying in effect, that from today all future history would be dated. And what is more, and even stranger to Jewish ears, they were claiming scriptural authority for what was taking place in Jerusalem (as Peter will say shortly, 'This is what was spoken by the prophet Joel') and declaring that the new age of prophetic hope and dream was actually here. So the remarkable thing about this *glossolalia*, unlike the use of 'tongues' elsewhere in Acts and 1 Corinthians, is its nature as instant communication, based on scriptural materials that are claimed as being fulfilled in the immediate experience of Christians. Luke's recital of a bevy of place names invites us to think of his 'theological geography' by which the spread of the gospel, predicted in Acts 1:8, will be ensured in the following years of the church's witness until Rome itself is won.

What Does It Mean?

The outer framework of the Pentecost story encloses even deeper meanings. These may now be listed as we continue to bear in mind something of Luke's purpose in giving the reader the details of what happened on the church's birthday. For Luke the Jerusalem community was the mother-church;[5] and very likely when he came to write up the story of the Jerusalem community it had been dispersed during the tumultuous years of AD 66–72 which saw the coming of Roman armies to quell the Jewish uprising and the destruction of the Temple. At the simplest level Luke wanted to acquaint Theophilus (see Acts 1:1; Luke 1:1–4) with the facts of past history by telling him what he should know regarding 'Christian origins.'

But Luke is no mere narrator of events in the distant past. Both his gospel and this second volume were written out of the conviction that the living Lord was still leading his people and that what Jesus did in Galilee, Samaria, and Jerusalem was but a beginning (see again Acts 1:1); moreover what the same risen Christ did in the lives of Peter and Paul, the heroes respectively of the two panels of Acts, chapters 1–12 and 13–28, he was continuing to do in the years that followed the apostolic martyrdoms in AD 65. It is not difficult to imagine that for Christians living in the few decades between AD 70 and the turn of the century one urgent issue would be: with the decease of the leading apostles how can we be sure of guidance and leadership in the church? Luke's answer is clear. The living Lord is present with his people by the Holy Spirit whose work is to contemporize that personal presence and to show how he is still going ahead of his people and strengthening them to do the very tasks he first assigned to the original apostles – to witness (Acts 1:8, 2:32, 5:32, 9:15, 20:24, 23:11) and to suffer for his sake (Acts 5:41, 8:1, 9:16, 22:17 etc.).

In these decades of opportunity and challenge the church saw the dispersal of the Jerusalem community, the increasing separation between church, now predominantly Gentile-oriented, and the Jewish synagogue,[6] and other problems associated with this inevitable time gap. These were the questions of the delay in the Lord's return in glory, the disappearance of apostolic figures from the scene and a mounting tendency for the church to become top-heavy with structures of organization, ministry and offices (witness the details of the Pastoral epistles). It was becoming clear that such a church would be in danger of *losing contact with the memory of its beginnings*. Luke intends to make good this defect lest the roots of the past should be severed and lost for all time.

Underlying Luke's concern was a deep pastoral regard. He was interested in relating the past not for its own sake, nor simply to hold up before his contemporaries a model to evoke their admiration and to satisfy their curiosity as to where the church came from when it appeared fresh and bright from the hands of its Lord. He was pointing to the early years in no spirit of nostalgia as though he were pining for 'good old days' that could never return. By the emphasis on the ever-present Lord and the dynamic Spirit whose power was released at every critical phase of the church's outward movement in the careers of Peter, Barnabas, Stephen, Apollos, and Paul, Luke was recalling the past that it might speak to the present; he was beckoning his contemporaries to re-live that experience by which the 'conquering new-born joy' of Pentecost is meant to be shared in every subsequent age.

If we hold this purpose of Luke's story steadily in view, the reader's understanding of these chapters in Acts will, we suggest, be more in line with their original intention; and it will assist us today to see what relevance there may be in the twentieth century. We proceed to tabulate the main features of the Lukan record.

a. Obviously the centre piece of the story is *the coming of the Holy Spirit*. The impressive build-up in the verses that set the scene, whether in the 'upper room' of Jerusalem (Acts 1:13, 2:1) or the Temple court which they later frequented (5:12), serves to focus on the main climactic event: 'they were all filled with the Holy Spirit' (2:4). The emphasis on the Spirit as a universal gift is meant to mark out this 'coming' from the spirit's activity in Israel's past history. Then at various times the 'spirit of the Lord' came and possessed the nation's leaders, the prophets and the wise men. But the people had to be content with a spirit-possessed leadership. Now, as a sign of the new age just ushered in, the divine spirit rests on the entire company, apostles and non-apostles alike, men and women without distinction, as Joel had promised (Acts 2:17,18). Moses' plea, when the prophesying of Eldad and Medad in the camp caused consternation to Joshua who advised they should be restrained, is exactly in line with the general situation in the Old Testament period. The spirit had rested on these men (Num. 11:26), though they did not belong to the company of the elders of Israel. Moses is generous in his assessment of what was happening, and looks to a day when it will be a normal occurrence. 'I wish that the Lord would give his spirit to all his people and make all of them shout like prophets!' That day, Luke is saying, has come. And come to stay.

The *abiding presence* of the Holy Spirit is a notable feature of the Pentecostal church. At least so we may infer from the absence of any hint to the contrary. The Spirit that descended and enriched the lives of the people whether leaders like Peter or others who included the women and the holy family members (Acts 1:14) as well as the 'brethren' of Acts 1:15, remained with them. Again the distinctiveness of the Spirit's relationship is markedly different from what we have in the Old Testament and intertestamental period. There the Lord's spirit comes and departs at will. The spirit possesses Saul, Israel's first king, but leaves him in distress (1 Sam. 16:14). Samson had earlier been stirred by the spirit (Judges 13:25); but the sad ending of his career stems from the fact that 'he did not know that the Lord had left him' (Judges 16:20). The later prophets knew the spirit as coming mightily upon them – but apparently only for some specific task and for a limited time (Micah 3:8).

It is different when the new age of salvation dawns. The great day brings the Spirit as the abiding possession of the church, since it is this Spirit that is to remain 'with you for ever' (John 14:16). Nor is there any suggestion that a renewed visitation of the Spirit at a later time (Acts 4:31) was needed because the Spirit had withdrawn in the meanwhile. Rather a fresh coming of the Spirit was experienced in response to the new needs of boldness and courage in bearing witness. Paul's teaching will later theologize these pointers in a clear statement in Romans 8:5–16 (compare Eph. 1:13,14, 4:30). His statement is undoubtedly based on the premise that the Spirit's presence is the enduring hallmark of the life and activity of the Christian and the church, as is clear from Galatians 3:2, 5:25.

Yet once more the narrative in Acts 2 draws attention to the descent of the Spirit as *a necessary prerequisite for Christian proclamation.* The activity of the Spirit is thus not an end in itself. The Johannine church was to receive this warning about the Paraclete: he will not speak 'from himself' (John 16:13). Rather the Spirit will declare the truth that will witness to Jesus and so 'glorify him' (John 16:14). It was precisely this function that made the witness of the Pentecostal company in Jerusalem so effective. Their united language, as God gave them a promised fulfilment of Isaiah 66:18 ('I am coming to gather all nations and tongues; and they shall come and see my glory'), was the vehicle of his 'mighty works,' and the focus of interest centred on what God had done – specifically he had raised up his Son from death to life (Acts 2:24) and installed him as head of the messianic fellowship (2:36). Peter's confirming witness (2:32) has its place. But the central thrust of the sermon is to demonstrate that Joel's prophecy of the Spirit's coming has brought fulfilment not to that scripture alone, or even the Old Testament prediction as an important item. The chief event to which the Spirit witnesses is the enthronement of Jesus, once crucified and now elevated to heaven's highest place. Right at the dawn of apostolic history it became clear that God's spirit is the Spirit of Jesus Christ. And there is no separate gospel of the Holy Spirit apart from the church's Lord and head.

b. Peter's message pierced the hearers' hearts like a rapier thrust. 'Brethren, what shall we do?' invited his response in terms of a call to repentance, baptism and forgiveness. The same Holy Spirit whose signs were plainly to be seen was promised to all who would accept Peter's offer; not surprisingly, we are told that there was a considerable response (Acts 2:37–41).[7]

The dawning of the messianic era which the Spirit's coming on the first followers of Jesus of Nazareth heralded was to see *the emergence of a new society.* What may have been dismissed as an ephemeral outbreak of religious excitement and emotional upheaval among a group of Jewish enthusiasts turns out to be something solid and permanent. The apostles' word is not primarily 'Come, catch our enthusiasm and share our joy.' It is rather, 'Come, join God's new society and take your place in its ranks.' There is an identifiable body of men and women, not just an amorphous collection of individuals, each professing a religious experience. So the key phrase is 'there were added to the group' (Acts 2:41) in the fresh accession of the three thousand who came to seek pardon and a place in the new world. The church at its grass-roots was already a fellowship committed to stay together. Any notion that believers in Jesus could or would live in 'solitary splendour' or apart from the group receives scant support from these chapters in Acts.

  c. Luke's picture of life in the Jerusalem 'mother church' has an appeal of its own. Not least is the *happy combination of flexibility and order*. There was a spontaneity felt as the Spirit moved across this company and directed their efforts at witness, evangelism and growth. That the Jerusalem Christians saw it as their first task to remain in the holy city and try to influence their Jewish compatriots in the hope that a national repentance would pave the way for the Gentiles to flock to Zion's hill (as promised in Isa. 2:1–3, 62:1,2; cf. Zech. 8:20–23, 14:16) seems clear from Acts 3:17–26, 5:29–32. The tragedy was that Israel refused this second chance to heed the claims of her messiah and remained obdurate (Rom. 10:21, 11:25). Luke passed no critical judgment on how this Jewish Christian church clung to a false hope; but the observant reader would see that the fuller revelation which came with Stephen, Philip and the hellenists of Acts 11:19–21 provided a clear pointer to where the church's future lay. The ground is being made ready for Saul who will carry the good news to those outside the Jewish fold and ultimately to the ends of the earth (Acts 1:8). *That* was Luke's heartfelt interest.

  Luke's purpose in these initial chapters is to present some cameo scenes of an idyllic community. Acts 2:42 may be taken as a summary statement:

> They spent their time in
> learning from the apostles,
> taking part in the fellowship,
> and sharing in the fellowship meals
> and the prayers.

  One notable study by the Scandinavian scholar Bo Reicke has suggestively called attention to the structure and meaning of this one verse as an epitome of Luke's record.[8] The four items listed as the activity of the Jewish Christian believers are arranged in two sets of matching couplets: the apostles' teaching and the prayers go together; fellowship and sharing in meals stand side by side. He goes on to suggest that we should see in the key word 'fellowship' (*koinōnia*) both an inward-looking dimension and also an outward-reaching emphasis. Later on we will look more closely at this important New Testament term, *koinōnia* rendered 'fellowship.' For the present it will be enough to accept Reicke's division as indicating the interest of Christians seen in the Jerusalem church.

They strengthened their grasp on the truth that underlay their experience by exploring what the apostles taught. Luke himself had cause to be grateful for access to this instruction when it came to collecting material for his gospel, since he refers to traditions handed down from 'eyewitnesses and ministers of the word' (Luke 1:2). There have been several proposals as to what this teaching may have contained: some see a ground plan of the life of Jesus in Peter's sermon to Cornelius in Acts 10:36–43.[9] Or else we may appeal to 1 Corinthians 15:3–5 where Paul is reciting an early confession of faith which he received from those who were Christians before he came on to the scene. There is evidence that this credo may well go back to some semitic-speaking church, possibly at Jerusalem. Other fragments of credal statements mentioned in Paul's letters have been placed in the setting of this early community, for instance Romans 3:24–26, 4:25 and 10:9. The use of Psalm 118:22 (quoted in Acts 4:11) put the emphasis on what pre-Pauline Christianity evidently made the centre of its teaching and preaching: Jesus was the rejected stone which is now honoured by being set as the keystone of the archway. The twin themes of Jesus' humiliation and death and his later vindication by God in the resurrection formed a large part of this message.

The definite article with the word 'prayers' suggests an observance of the Jewish hours of devotion within the framework of the Temple liturgy. This is exactly what we find in the story of Acts 3:1–10. Peter and John visit the Temple court at the afternoon hour of prayer. Luke has a special attachment to the Jerusalem Temple, for his gospel opens (1:8) as it closes (24:53) in the setting of the holy place. He is at pains to show how the first disciples ordered their devotional life within the framework of Judaic institutions, especially the Temple service (see Acts 2:46, 5:12, 5:42). The more informal house gatherings are not overlooked, but it is perhaps more significant that there was in Luke's mind an attachment to the ordered pattern of corporate worship provided by the Temple and its liturgy.

The 'centrifugal' movement of their *koinōnia*, as Reicke calls it, is measured by an outgoing concern for the physical and social wellbeing of those in need. Centred on the love-feast or agape-meal and serviced by a common fund to which contributions were made, this social activity sprang directly from a concern to provide for the destitute, as we see from Acts 6:1. Later famine conditions in AD 46–48 (referred to in Acts 11:28–30) only exacerbated the difficulty and gave rise to the designation found in Paul, 'the poor among the saints in Jerusalem' (Rom. 15:26; 2 Cor. 9:12). These people Paul was only too ready to help (Gal. 2:10).

The exact relationship between the love-meal with a shared table and what later became known as the solemn 'communion' service is not clear. Evidently by the time of the writing of 1 Corinthians in AD 54 the two services could be separated and the effect of Paul's counsel was to downplay the common meal because of excesses (1 Cor. 11:17–22,33,34). The consequence of this recommendation was to put the chief emphasis on the service that focused on the Lord's death and to preface that service not with a social meal but a preparation involving self-scrutiny and a thoughtful approach to the sacred meal (1 Cor. 11:28,29).

What does bind together the Jerusalem table fellowship and the Pauline model is a common insistence on *koinōnia*. This is expressed in a practical concern for one's neighbour and his wellbeing. The common fund and the shared table are examples in Luke's writing of such Christian interest.

d. Our cursory sketch would be incomplete without a passing reference to *the sense of wonder and awe* that apparently pervaded the scene. More than one verse in these chapters highlights the realization of the divine presence which drew near (2:43, 3:10, 5:11,13). The reality of the 'numinous,' giving a sense of holy fear in the presence of God's holiness, finds sharp focus in the judgment story of Ananias and his wife (Acts 5:1–11). The leading theme of the account is the voluntary nature of the sacrifices which people made as they brought their gifts to the common purse. So Ananias' sin was not that he failed to give everything. Clearly it was his choice whether he would do so or not (Acts 5:4). His terrible mistake was to attempt a deceit by pretending to give all when he and Sapphira had colluded in a scheme to retain part of their property for themselves. The occasion of the fearful judgment-sentence was their hypocrisy and pretence, not their covetousness. And from Peter's stern words they were evidently intent on practising deceit even when they had a chance to own up. Probably what moved Luke to add a judgment story like this was not a love of anecdotal material nor a morbid interest in a summary execution nor even a desire to record a lesson in salutary discipline. He is honest enough to tell 'the other side' of the church's early life, the bad as well as the good; and he records the fate of this couple as a warning of a fearful deed that marred the new creation which like the old order of creation had come fresh from its maker's hand.[10] The term 'church' (5:11) is found here for the first time in Acts, as though to underscore that point.

3
Fellowship: The Anatomy of a Word

What's in a Name?

Among the handful of words that may be regarded as key terms of the Bible, 'fellowship' holds an important place. Indeed it is a 'buzz' word in modern Christianity as expressed among young people's groups and movements. We all use it often, sometimes without a second thought as to its full sense or deep meaning. Clearly it played a central part in the lexicon of the early Christians, as a glance at any Bible concordance or word-list will show. Our task is to pass a representative selection of these occurrences under quick review and see what their meaning was for the New Testament writers. Then we shall be in a position to read off the application of the word for our situation today.

In recent years important soundings of the word 'fellowship' have been taken, and we are happily in a position to hear more distinctly the overtones of meaning the first Christians gave to it.[1] At least three nuances are perceptible, and they provide us with the pattern of our study.

But first we can reflect on the setting of the church in Jerusalem. As Acts 2:42 reminds us, they gave careful attention to 'the fellowship.' Whether this could possibly be claimed as a self-description of believers, perhaps antedating the word 'church' and then obviously preceding in time the coining of the familiar title, 'Christian' (see Acts 11:26) is debated. It is just possible that the term 'fellowship' was boldly appropriated and taken over from the Jewish synagogues where an equivalent Hebrew term was used of the enclave of pietistic Jews known as the Pharisees. What we are observing in this transition is a rebirth of the Jewish ideal of a 'holy people.' The followers of Jesus looked upon themselves as a christianized version of this 'separated' group,

34

devoted to God and his will. The Pharisaic term *haburah* is pressed into service, and the devotees of the messiah were conscious of an identity as a 'fellowship' united by a common allegiance to Jesus in whom they had believed as God's anointed one.

This is possible, especially if it is true that the Pharisees thought of themselves not as a movement within Israel but the embodiment of the true Israel. This is precisely the way the early church saw its role. But there are some objections, not least that all we know of the ethos and way of life of these Christian societies marks them out as differing from the Pharisees in such practices as observing the laws of ritual cleanness and so committed to Jewish exclusivism. The accusation brought against their leaders is precisely that they were ignorant of the finer points of rabbinical learning and were associated more with the 'people of the land' whom the Pharisees despised (Acts 4:13; see John 7:49).

If we want an introduction to these men and women in terms that they themselves used, we shall do better to seek it in the distinctively Christian language used in Acts. The phrases concerned are 'the friends' (4:23) or 'those of the way' (9:2, 22:4, 24:22). In the eyes of the Jewish hierarchy they were known to be a 'sect' (Acts 24:5, 28:22), a religious group within the framework of Judaism, holding unusual beliefs. But in their own eyes they were 'the saints' (Acts 9:13, 26:10; Rom. 15:25,26; 2 Cor. 8:4, 9:1 etc.) who belonged to Jesus the Christ, distinguished more by dedication to him than by separation from their fellows. Devotion to the risen Lord was the hallmark of their way of life; and the living, dynamic expression of what the life-in-Christ meant is seen in clear focus as we study all that is involved in 'fellowship.'

Two preliminary remarks are to be made, once we have surveyed the data and before we attempt an arrangement of those data into a pattern. First, there is no full understanding of *koinōnia* in the Old Testament revelation. The word itself and its associated terms are only rarely found in the Old Testament translation in Greek called the Septuagint; and when the term is used in those books originally written in Greek it never designates any communion between God and man. Occasionally there may be a union between man and a divine attribute such as his wisdom (Wisdom of Solomon 6:23, 8:18), but awareness of the transcendence of God kept any sense of intimate fellowship with him a remote possibility.

Secondly, in the world of the Greeks the word is used so expansively as to lose much of its precise shape. It covers all types of common enterprise from the marriage union between husband and wife to a bond of human friendship, 'a mixing of souls.' Sometimes men are thought to share in the life of the gods but more in the manner of a union than of a conscious, reciprocal communion.

From these observations and the few (but important) references in Acts and the letters of Peter and John in the later New Testament, we conclude that teaching on fellowship is pre-eminently that of Paul. It is to his writings we must look for a formulation of what 'fellowship' means, and it is he who employs the word as 'one of the many ways in Scripture of expressing the central Christian mystery, the union in love of God and man through Jesus Christ.'[2] As such it may be claimed to be 'the main theme of Christianity,'[3] at least in its Pauline expression.

Having a Share

The root idea of koinōnia is 'taking part in something with someone.' At once we are faced with the question of emphasis: in that thumbnail definition, which is more important to the biblical authors, the realities in which Christians share or the sense of sharing that binds them to one another? We are alerted right away to a practical issue, for in our modern parlance we give the chief place usually to the second part of the definition and underline the phrase 'with someone' often at the expense of the first words. We think of fellowship as our being together in the company of others in prayer or worship or on some social venture. This is what makes our 'fellowship' real! But, as we shall see, the New Testament puts the emphasis on the 'in something' aspect, and invariably the stress falls on the privilege which comes to us as we join with other Christians in participation in 'objective realities,' outside and independent of our experience because they are there before we lay hold of them and they exist irrespective of our feelings. This becomes crystal clear as we look at some texts in Paul.

a. 'God is to be trusted, the God who called you to have fellowship with his Son Jesus Christ, our Lord' (1 Cor. 1:9).

God is praised by Paul as the one who initiates the union between himself and the church, a union called 'the fellowship of his Son Jesus Christ our Lord.' Faced with a fragmented congregation, split into rival factions (1 Cor. 1:10–13, 3:4) Paul affirms the place of true unity. It is the common life shared by all believers on the ground that they all, by their calling as Christians, participate in Jesus Christ. How they do so is not clear, whether it is in a mystical way as Deissmann believed, coining the phrase 'a genitive of fellowship' to explain the words at the end of the verse, or in a realistic manner as though Paul were talking of the Corinthians' 'becoming-one-with' the risen Lord (as 1 Cor. 6:17). What is clear is the reality of Jesus Christ as the 'one Lord' (1 Cor. 8:6) in whom the church is one because all its members are united with him. At the outset Paul strikes a blow at all divisiveness and party-groupings, and insists on the church's unity. Thus *koinōnia* becomes the 'ruling idea of the entire letter,'[4] just as 1 John 1:3 sets the same tone for that letter in a less obviously polemical context.

b. 'Do you have fellowship with the Spirit?' (RSV 'So if there is . . . any participation in the Spirit') (Phil. 2:1).

This preface to a call to Christian unity also confronts the sad situation of a church broken by discord and strife. The Philippians are being summoned to a better way. In his typical manner Paul first lays a groundwork for his imperative by a statement of what is true: 'If, as is the case, there is any fellowship of the Spirit.'

The commentators have puzzled over Paul's meaning, since his Greek words may be taken in two senses. Is he appealing to a fellowship produced by the Spirit, either by promoting the church's unity or joining believers to the Lord? Or is Paul grounding his appeal to the Philippians on their 'participation in the Spirit,' the objective genitive? A moment's reflection will surely suggest the second interpretation as preferable. Paul could have used the normal term for 'unity' if he had the first idea in mind, (a thought already given in Phil. 1:27) and the surrounding context of the verse (2:1) clinches the point that it is the objective reality of the Holy Spirit in whom the church lives in communion that provides the solid basis for Paul's apostolic directive which follows in 2:2-4.

We are united with the Godhead in the persons of the Son and Spirit. (Paul never uses the term 'fellowship with God' though John does.) It is not surprising then that Paul would want to pray for a continuing and deepening of that 'participation in the Holy Spirit' in the lives of his people (2 Cor. 13:13) since they are the people of God, made such by sharing in his divine life (Heb. 6:4) which is none other than 'the life of God in the souls of men.' Now we are sharers in the divine nature (2 Pet. 1:4) in hope of a fuller realization of what that means in an eschatological future (1 Pet. 5:1).

 c. 'Thankful for your partnership in the gospel from the first day until now' (Phil. 1:5).

The same Philippian church meant much to the apostle. He speaks of them in terms of endearment and affection (4:1). In the preamble of his letter Paul is thankful to God for their 'fellowship in the gospel' from the first days of his initial evangelism in their city (Acts 16:12–40) right up to the present. During the interim he has received help from this church repeatedly (Phil. 4:14–18). Exactly how he viewed that support is the theme of his opening remarks: he is grateful for their remembrance of him (1:3) expressed in the way they had proved that they were one in the gospel ministry along with him. True, it appears at first glance that their partnership (koinōnia) is with Paul, but 1:7 makes it clear that the 'grace' in which they are partners is a divine activity and Paul is just as much a sharer in God's grace as they are.

So 1:7 has to mean: you and I share together in God's grace. I share in the privilege of the apostolic ministry, and you too share in it with me by your faithful and costly (2 Cor. 8:1–5) support. Already we are beginning to see how *koinōnia* shades off into a partnership that takes on concrete form by Christian giving.[5]

d. '[You Gentiles] now share the strength and rich life of the Jews' (Rom. 11:17).

In discharging his missionary responsibility Paul never allowed his debt to Israel to drop from his view. Always he lives in a constant tension between his concern for his nation, the Jews, and his desire to fulfil the destiny of Isaiah's servant of the Lord who was to be 'a light to the Gentiles' (Isa. 49:6, quoted in Acts 13:47). Romans 9:1–5, 10:1 could have been written only by a man for whom this dual responsibility was an acutely sensitive matter.

Equally Paul taught his Gentile converts to respect their indebtedness to ethnic Israel as God's people. Apparently some of them were despising the Jewish background of their new faith since they had come to Christ out of a pagan milieu. Paul, like all the other New Testament writers, strove to contradict this false idea, namely that Christians in non-Jewish communities can cut themselves free from their Old Testament heritage. 'Do not despise those who were the people of God under the old covenant' is Paul's warning (Rom. 11:18). The reason has just been given. Gentile believers are sharers in the rich inheritance that has come to them in the family of Abraham's children. In that family both believing Jews and converted Gentiles take their place (Rom. 3:29,30, 4:12; Gal. 3:26–29, 4:28–31).

e. 'We know that just as you share in our sufferings, you also share in the help we receive' (2 Cor. 1:7).

The same apostle who entered upon a lifetime of service at the behest of the living Lord quickly came to realise that this vocation was no easy sinecure. A life of suffering and hardship awaited him, as Ananias was quick to warn him in advance (Acts 9:16). The catalogue of Paul's apostolic privations and persecutions in 2 Corinthians 11:23–29 makes painful reading if we allow our imagination to flesh out the details of what he summarily describes both here and in other places (e.g. Gal. 6:17).

Yet it is vital to recall that Paul's sufferings were not endured by him in a 'private' capacity as though he were a lawbreaker deserving punishment or a social misfit receiving the reaction of an unsympathetic and hostile world around him. The opening of 2 Corinthians makes it obvious that Paul was experiencing in his affliction in Asia – and it brought him to death's door (2 Cor. 1:8,9) – no less than Christ's sufferings. In some undefined but realistic manner Paul was entering into the 'travail of the messiah' (a Jewish idea which is in the background of Col. 1:24) and the Lord and the apostle were in it together, just as Christ identified himself with the sufferings of his people (Acts 9:4; 1 Cor. 8:12).

Moreover the joint participation in which messiah and messianic apostle share extends to messiah's people. The Corinthians are linked with Paul's sufferings for their sake, and at the outset of a letter whose master theme is the humiliation and vulnerability of Paul's apostleship these people who had despised Paul's lowly, unassuming and unimpressive bearing are reminded that they too have a share in a vocation that is patterned on the lowly Jesus (2 Cor. 10:1) who came to his glory along a pathway of weakness (2 Cor. 13:4) and costly obedience to the Father's will. For what it cost Paul to live by this truth, 2 Corinthians 4:7–12 should be pondered.

In Philippians 3:10 he calls the experience 'a sharing in his sufferings, becoming thereby like him in his death.' We may set aside any idea that Paul thought of himself, here or at Colossians 1:24, as a saviour figure, making up an incomplete atonement. Never does Paul hint that the cross of Jesus was insufficient. Equally he is not advocating a mystical union set up by Christ's sufferings, though the Christian saints and martyrs for the faith have discovered a vivid community of fellow-feeling that has joined them to the suffering Christ. Rather it is Paul's way of expressing a close identity which is not quite a becoming one with the dying Lord. 'Becoming like him' in his death means a vivid experience of entering into the spirit of the humiliated Christ, a renouncing of all privilege and pretension of greatness, an acceptance of his low estate of poverty (2 Cor. 8:9) and loss, a detachment from worldly standards and aspirations, and a glad embrace of God's will as sovereign even when it runs counter to human preferences and pleasures (Mark 14:32–36).

This is a tall order. Who is adequate for such a calling? asks Paul (2 Cor. 2:16). The motive power is the resurrection power of the same Lord who provides strength and help (RSV in 2 Cor. 1:7, 'comfort' is slightly misleading) to enable our *koinōnia* to be realistically faced and accepted, even with joy and expectation. (See Heb. 10:33–36 for a notable illustration of how such 'sharing in loss' can be turned to good account. The exiled John in Rev. 1:9 offers another noble example of shared suffering that is transformed into the confidence of a coming victory.)

f. 'The cup of blessing for which we give thanks to God: do we not share in the blood of Christ when we drink from this cup? And the bread we break: do we not share in the body of Christ when we eat this bread?' (1 Cor. 10:16).

In both instances the expected answer is yes. For the eating and drinking (as we reverse Paul's order to our more familiar sequence) are acts of obedience, faith and love by which we participate in the realities represented by and in a measure conveyed through the bread and the wine. 'For Paul the bread and wine are vehicles of the presence of Christ . . . . Partaking of bread and wine is union (sharing) with the heavenly Christ . . . . *koinōnia* is here expressive of an inner union. This is for Paul the important thing in the celebration.'[6] Provided we include the element of faith as the means by which the participation in Christ and his presence are achieved and experienced – as Hauck does in a preceding sentence – this succinct statement may stand, and in a later chapter we shall look more closely at the nature of Christ's presence at the supper meal of the church.

For the moment we note again the insistence on the objective realities to which our faith in Christ joins us. The body and blood of Christ stand for his sacrifice in life and death and his risen power. He lived the perfect life of obedience; he died the vicarious death; he was raised to be his people's advocate. All of this is true outside of our experience. Yet we are called to be sharers in those tangible elements of bread and cup that speak so eloquently of these invisible yet real entities.

In the context of 1 Corinthians the table of the Lord is the focal point of unity, so that there can be no justification for the Corinthians' squabbling when they 'all share the same loaf' (10:17). On a wider canvas the participation in Christ's body and blood are the pilgrim's sustenance in trial, since the church faces the sharing of Christ's suffering in the knowledge that his risen presence is there as often as the bread is broken and the cup poured (Luke 24:28–35; Acts 10:41) and the celebration under the sign of the cross in this age points forward to the greater rejoicing at the messianic banquet of the age to come (1 Cor. 11:26, 16:22; Rev. 19:7–9).

Giving a Share

So far we have looked at verses and passages, chiefly in Paul, that direct our attention to the 'good things' in which we have a share. 'Good,' that is, not necessarily in the sense of pleasant and delightful but rather as God's gifts to his people.

But 'good things' are meant to be shared and spread around to others. So it happens in a natural transference of meaning that *koinōnia* shades off from 'participation in' to include 'sharing with' another person or a group. The obvious translation for this dimension of fellowship is *generosity* or *community*. In both cases the fellowship with others on the basis of the common life in which we and they share – and that proviso is important – takes on tangible, concrete and often sacrificial expression. It is more than mere sentiment or kindly feeling; it assumes the quantifiable shape of a gift or a contribution.

> *a.* 'Many will give glory to God . . . for your generosity in sharing with them and all others' (2 Cor. 9:13).

This verse should be read in conjunction with 2 Corinthians 8:4; and both should then be compared with Romans 15:26. In each instance the subject is the same. Paul is concerned to honour the pledge he gave to the Jerusalem church leaders (Gal. 2:10) to 'remember the poor.' These were the poverty-stricken saints of the mother church, in dire straits on account of the severe famine in Judaea in the mid-forties (Acts 11:28–30). Throughout the churches of his planting in Macedonia and southern Greece Paul was, ten years later, busy raising a relief fund.

2 Corinthians 8:4 praises the *koinōnia* the Macedonians displayed: they wanted to assist the saints in Judaea in their need, even though the givers themselves were in great financial stress. The Corinthians are summoned to follow this splendid example and to show generosity by 'the integrity of your fellowship (or, your participation [in the collection])' as C. K. Barrett renders 9:13.[7]

The third reference takes on an even more down-to-earth dress. 'Fellowship' in Rom. 15:26 is 'clearly used in the sense of "collection." '[8] Paul is evidently in these three texts piling up expressions such as 'generosity,' 'service,' 'sincerity' for the sake of effect and intending to enforce the single thought of the Christians' concern for those in need. 'Fellowship' is a fourth term in this cluster with a nuance borrowed from its partners. It serves to underscore the requirement that any claim to partnership with others must take on a practical shape; otherwise it evaporates into an expression of mere well-wishing, of which James writes so scathingly (James 2:14–17) and which John denounces with no less feeling (1 John 3:17,18).

b. 'They spent their time . . . taking part in the fellowship' (Acts 2:42).

So we return to the primitive church on its Pentecostal foundation. The suggestion is offered that this summarizing verse gives an epitome of early church life and describes the various aspects of its liturgical service. If this way of viewing the verse has any plausibility, and instruction, eucharistic meals and prayers are the ingredients of its cultic exercise, then 'fellowship' could stand for the taking of the collection. It is appropriate that the next paragraph in Luke's record goes on to speak of the believers' 'sharing their belongings with one another' (2:44) – a quality of life whose features are repeated in 4:32, they held all things as common property (*koina*). Out of this fund, as we observed, gifts were made to the needy.

This interpretation is plausible, but not certain. Probably we shall do better to keep the term 'fellowship' in Acts 2:42 for describing the believers' common life together, while not denying that they did exhibit a caring attitude for one another that expressed itself in compassionate and concrete forms. This expression of their new life would take on fresh meaning, even if most of them had learned as a duty from the cradle the Jewish obligation to 'show kindness' to the poor and needy. Rabbi Simeon had coined the dictum centuries before that the world stands on a platform with three feet: 'the Law, the Worship and the showing of kindness.' This is not a bad summary of the ethos of Jewish Christianity as we meet it in the early chapters of Acts. The 'handing-out of kindnesses' refers to just those acts of compassion, generosity and concern for others that Jews demonstrate as the practical application of religion. The new dimension that Jesus brought to prominence was a concern for one's neighbour when he happens to be a Samaritan (Luke 10:25–37) or a foreigner or persons really outside our 'set' (Matt. 25:31–46).

We all need guidance in the exercise of our stewardship. Paul's final word neatly sums the competing claims on our generosity that we often feel: 'The man who is being taught the Christian message should share (*koinōneitō*) all the good things he has with his teacher' (Gal. 6:6: in modern terms, support the clergy and ministers of the word); 'As often as we have the chance we should do good to everyone, and especially to those who belong to our family in the faith' (Gal. 6:10).

Embodying a Shared Life

Just a few places in the New Testament have the word *koinōnia* on its own, without any following terms associated with it. It has been suggested that in these cases the most suitable rendering would be 'fellowship, in the sense of partnership or joint participation in a common enterprise.'[9] Galatians 2:9 is a case in point. There the 'right hand of fellowship' extended to Paul and Barnabas implied that they were accepted as partners in the task of proclaiming the gospel, whether it was to Jews or non-Jews.

Acts 2:42 may carry this idea also, depending on how we understand the term in association with the other key words used to describe early church life. Certainly 'partnership in a common enterprise' would fill the bill admirably; as also in 1 John 1:3: '. . . you may have fellowship with us. And our fellowship is with the Father.'

Here the life of the church is in view, seen as a shared or common life which is connected by the sinews and tissues of interdependence and mutuality. But the thought is much more that of drawing strength from God than of mutual support and comfort. The 'shared life' depends primarily on God who by his Spirit joins the separate believers together. To that work of the Holy Spirit we devote our next chapter.

4
Charismatic Gifts: Who Needs Them?

A Fellowship of the Holy Spirit

The church is the community of the risen Lord since it is by union with him that God's life flows into those who make up the company called by this name. It is none the less the fellowship of the Holy Spirit since it is the work of the Spirit to make real the presence of Jesus Christ in everyday experience. He is the 'go-between God,' as John V. Taylor's title reminds us,[1] who unites men and women to God-in-Christ as he actualizes God's reality in Jesus Christ to those persons in their contemporary experience.

In several places, Paul discusses the new life that came to his Gentile congregations. Possibly the earliest reference is Galatians 3:1–5 which is centred on the pointed question: 'Did you receive God's Spirit . . . by hearing and believing in the gospel?' (verse 2). That direct question is answered by Paul later in the letter, though the affirmative reply is inferred from its context. He leaves his readers in no doubt at Galatians 5:25, 'The Spirit has given us life'; then he sounds a warning note, 'He must also control our lives.' Claiming to have the Spirit is one thing – and Paul would not doubt it; but for him what matters is the evidence that, when 'God gives you the Spirit and works miracles among you' (Gal. 3:5), 'the fruit of the Spirit' is visible according to the cluster of qualities listed in Galatians 5:22,23.

In 1 Thessalonians, which is another 'early' letter of Paul, at least in the sense that it was composed and sent off to a recently founded congregation, we find the same linkage between 'experience' and 'evidence.' Almost casually, Paul can write of God's work in the midst of the people of Thes-

salonica that he is 'at work in you who believe' (2:13) because
'God . . . gives you his Holy Spirit' (4:8). The giving of the
Spirit was God's answer to their believing, while their receiving Paul's message as God's word was in turn an activity of
'the Spirit's power to make you God's own people' (2 Thess.
2:13) since they came to faith only as he called them to
possess a share of the 'glory of our Lord Jesus Christ' (2
Thess. 2:14). In the context of the earlier paragraph the gift
of the divine Spirit was directed specifically to empower these
people to accept God's claim on their lives: 'This is what
God wants for you: to be holy . . . . God did not call us to
live in immorality, but in holiness' (1 Thess. 4:3,7). The same
emphasis is made: you are to be God's people, and the quality
of your life is shown by how you understand the gift of the
Holy Spirit. For (in the words of a later age) he is the Spirit
'who sanctifieth me and all the elect people of God.'[2]

The cautionary note sounded in Galatians is heard again
in Thessalonians, but in a different context. 'Do not restrain
the Holy Spirit' (1 Thess. 5:19) evidently implies that the
congregational leaders were alert to possible unseemly manifestations of the Spirit, perhaps in utterances that claimed to
be inspired and needed testing (verses 20,21). These out-
breaks were being kept in check and monitored.

In the church life at Corinth no such restraining influence
was present. The Christians there were not slow in telling
Paul that they had received special endowments; and he
gladly acknowledged this fact (1 Cor. 1:4,5,7). He conceded
that this was a congregation that was 'eager to have the gifts
of the Spirit' (1 Cor. 14:12) and to set its sights on excelling
in the life of the Spirit (1 Cor. 12:31). There was no shortage
of enthusiasm at Corinth. Quite the reverse. Interest in and
experience of the Spirit was greatly in evidence. The apostle
was more concerned to relate this kind of evidence to the
moral demands of the gospel and the distinctive life of the
Christian as a member of God's holy people, 'saints by calling' (1 Cor. 1:2).

Paul's response to a latent question about the 'spiritual
gifts' (*charismata*) is directed to the fundamental concern of
his apostolic ministry: what is it that makes the *charismata*
authentic, and how can believers set them in a right order of

priority and use these gifts of the Spirit worthily? The way he writes his introductory sentence (1 Cor. 12:1) shows that he has been approached by the Corinthians who were seeking an answer. The query may have been raised through reports sent from Chloe's family (1 Cor. 1:11) or perhaps through the delegation of their own members (1 Cor. 16:17). His reply is given in three chapters of 1 Corinthians 12–14;[3] and it falls into four parts. But before we examine what Paul says about the gifts of the Spirit, we must consider an even more basic issue.

The Gift of the Spirit

Paul's opening remark is meant to stab his readers awake. 'I want you to know the truth about [spiritual gifts], my brothers' (12:1). It is obviously not enough to have an experience of the Spirit or to receive what are claimed as his 'endowments-by-grace,' which is what *charismata* means. There is need to understand and believe and practise *the truth* about them. In other words, this opening statement is important as the apostle's reminder that not every claim to religious experience, spiritual ecstasy or wonder-working power is necessarily Christian. There are good spirits – and the Holy Spirit is par excellence the gracious indwelling power of God in his children, as Paul had taught them earlier in this letter (3:16, 6:19). But there are also demonic spirits that induce ecstasy and lead people astray, as the Corinthians were once misguided (12:2). Paul had already mentioned these malign forces in a previous discussion (10:20,21).

He has the readers' pre-Christian life in view. At that time they were in the grip of spiritual powers, no less real even though they should now realize that these 'demons' had no true existence: 'We know that an idol stands for something that does not really exist: we know that there is only the one God' (1 Cor. 8:4). Formerly they were in error and practised the worship of these dumb deities. 'Dumb' that is, in the sense of Psalm 115:4–8: the pagan gods were dead and unreal though powerful in the imagination and fear of the devotee. They even 'spoke' through their prophets and priestesses like the python or Sybil (see Acts 16:16). Pagan divinities often induced their followers into a state of trance and religious rapture. 'Mystical experience' can be found in most religions, and there is nothing uniquely Christian in either a yoga-like meditation or hallucinatory visions or glossolalic utterances.

One particular utterance must have been as offensive to Paul as to us today. In a religious ecstasy – when the human spirit was thought to be at prayer, but the mind had no part in it, to use the distinction of 1 Corinthians 14:14 – some member of the Corinthian assembly uttered the oath 'Jesus be damned!' (12:3, 'a curse on Jesus' is another translation). Worse still, that member attributed his cry to the Holy Spirit. But, Paul sharply retorts, this cannot be so, for the Holy Spirit leads no one to utter an uncontrolled blasphemy. Rather it is his work to inspire the words of what we may recognize as the earliest Christian confession of faith, 'Jesus is Lord', corresponding to the Jewish credo of Deuteronomy 6:4. To say from the heart that 'Jesus is Lord' is to enter into Christian salvation (Rom. 10:9,10). At worship, which is an anticipation of the end-time when God's kingdom will come in its fulness, the praise that unites all parts of creation is 'Jesus Christ is Lord' (Phil. 2:9–11). And for believers who need to be recalled to the first days of their new life-in-Christ the reminder is: 'Since you have accepted Christ Jesus as Lord, live in union with him' (Col. 2:6). Here is the badge of early Christianity. Christians were banded together under the motto, '*Jesus* is Lord'; not some pagan deity (1 Cor. 8:5,6), not some Roman emperor like Domitian who claimed honour as 'lord and god' (Rev. 1:6, 19:16), and not some bogus messiah who might arise with pretensions of grandeur and power (Mark 13:21,22; 2 Thess. 2:9,10).

False messiahs, heralded by false prophets and approved by pseudo-church leaders, were later to appear. But already in the Pauline and Johannine church circles these warnings were addressed to a present scene, as is clear from 2 Corinthians 11:4, 12–15 and 1 John 4:1–6. Just as Paul had to contend with 'false apostles,' 'the devil's servants,' so John warned of the presence in the midst of his church of 'false prophets . . . who belong to the world.' It is just possible that a common error runs through this type of aberrant Christianity which claimed to be Christian (1 John 2:19) but denied the profound truth of a historical incarnation. These men professed an attachment to Christ, but tried to sever Christ from the Jesus who lived a truly human life. John clearly exposed this as denying what is the heart of the Christian faith: God became man. For Paul this idea of a heavenly Christ divorced from the human Jesus (who was disowned in the cry, 'Jesus be damned') is nothing less than 'a different Jesus, not the one we preached.' Similarly, the claim that it is the Spirit who inspired the Corinthian cry is specious: it is 'a spirit . . . completely different from the Spirit' of our gospel (2 Cor. 11:4).[4]

To fall into christological error was bad enough. But at Corinth and in the Asian churches of John that was not all. Wrong-headed notions imagined the Christ to be a glorious, superhuman, majestic figure not related to the earthly Jesus whose feet touched our earth and who knew human weakness, temptation and suffering to the point of death. From this premise the false teachers deduced that the Christian life was equally exalted and power-laden, exempt from trial and loss and defeat. Judged by that criterion Paul's ministry showed up in a poor light, for his apostolic career was anything but a story of worldly success (2 Cor. 4:7–12, 11:21–12:10). But this standard is not Paul's, nor is it the pattern set by the life and death of Jesus. He was put to death on the cross in weakness (2 Cor. 13:4) before being raised in strength. The spirit he gave to his disciples was one of strength-in-weakness; the treasure of his message is contained in the fragile pots of clay; the life of his people is one of dying to live, as his life was. So both Paul and John draw a similar conclusion. As with the Lord, so with his church. There is no confession of Jesus Christ that divides the earthly, lowly Jesus from the exalted, regal Lord. There is no life-in-Christ that can know the triumph of his grace except along a path of humble discipleship – accepting the cross before gaining the crown (2 Cor. 4:11,12,17; John 13:1–20; 1 John 4:11).

To have the Spirit is to confess the faith of Christ crucified. To attest 'Jesus is Lord' is to live under the lordship of him who came to his throne along the road of costly obedience and lowly service (Mark 10:45; Luke 22:27). How may we evaluate the charismatic gifts? To do so, we must start at the cross to which Jesus came and where he says, 'Follow me' (Mark 8:34–37). We must recognize that the hallmark of the life-in-the-Spirit can never be divorced from the character of the earthly Jesus. The fruits of the Spirit are the virtues of Jesus. The 'kindness and gentleness of Christ' (2 Cor. 10:1) are the yardstick by which to measure all claims to enjoy the Spirit's gifts.[5]

Now perhaps we can look back and appreciate why the 'gift of the Spirit' is the key to the 'gifts of the Spirit.' We will never begin to grasp Paul's thinking about the *charismata* until we first see the importance of the Spirit's initial ministry: to lead men and women to the confession, 'Jesus is Lord.' This is his first and chiefest task: 'He will speak about me . . . he will give me glory' (John 15:26, 16:14). The Spirit's witness to the Lord and the Spirit's witness to our spirits (Rom. 8:16) are alike conducted in terms of his making real the person of Jesus Christ who is both earthly figure and exalted Lord. To relate these two aspects, and to live in the tension of 'weak, yet strong,' given in Paul's autobiography (2 Cor. 10:1, 12:10), is the genius of New Testament Christianity.

The Gifts of the Spirit

What are more properly called *charismata*, 'gifts-in-grace' or endowments of the Holy Spirit to the church, are the concern of Paul's extended treatment in 1 Corinthians 12:4–11. It is a serious mistake to detach this section from its setting in Paul's Corinthian correspondence and try to view it on its own. If ever a passage needed to be understood in relation to a pastoral situation it is this one, for clearly Paul is giving guidelines of instruction relating to a particular church problem. Part of that problem is an attitude that sees the Christian message as directed to an elite membership and boasts of its superior standing, its ecstatic experiences, its access to wonder-working powers. At the other end (we learn in 1 Cor. 12:12,13) the church family at Corinth needed to be reminded of its baptism 'into the one body by the same Spirit' and its constitution as a single body of Christ, though made up of many parts or organs. The intervening verses are bracketed by Paul's confronting these related problems.

a. The inclusive scope of the Spirit's gifts is made clear throughout. Notice how Paul deals with the question of spiritual pride that gave rise to cliques and party divisions: he insists that all Christians as believers and members of Christ's body are indwelt, baptized and watered by the Spirit (verses 1,13). By that token every believer is the recipient of some endowment which fits him or her for useful service within the fellowship. So we read: 'God gives ability to everyone' (verse 6); 'the Spirit's presence is shown in some way in each person' (verse 7); 'He gives a different gift to each person' (verse 11).

This feature stamps the Christian church as a social institution unique in the world. It is a society in which ideally every member has a part to play and a task to perform. Everyone in the church is important – irrespective of what social scientists call stratification (and the church at Corinth *was* socially diverse as we may see from passages which speak of the rich and the poor, 11:18–34, and define the general social status of most of the members, 1:26). Although no one is indispensable, there is a niche for each individual.

b. The rich variety of the Spirit's gifts is displayed by the phrase 'varieties of gifts' (verse 4: 'different kinds' is colourless as a rendering), all of which are attributed to the same Spirit. All Christians have some gift; but all do not have the same gift. In grace as in nature there is diversity and manifold variety.

The central verses of our passage (8–10) enumerate nine specimen 'workings' of the Spirit in the life of the apostolic congregations. We may immediately recognize some as continually in demand for the church's life in every age: gifts of wisdom, of knowledge, of proclamation have a timeliness and importance that makes them needed at every period of church history. By the same token, as there are gifts of permanent validity and value when assessed by the criterion of applicability and need, other items in Paul's list appear not to bear this hallmark of constant usefulness *in every circum-*

stance of the church's life. Hence while proclamation is a perennial need for the communicating of God's message, miracle-working, healing power, glossolalic speech and its interpretation may be gifts that recede for a while and then are renewed according to the needs of the hour.

The danger in lumping these nine gifts into a single package and treating them as equally intended for all ages is twofold. On the one hand, we may forget that the Spirit is our contemporary and he fashions *new* gifts for the church's ministry in every fresh setting and challenge of its life. On the other side, we fall guilty to the charge of theological anachronism when we suppose that modern-day Christianity in attempting to recapture its early days can reproduce in precise detail the conditions of its pristine life. To recall and re-live the spirit in which the first believers lived and served their generation is one thing, and may be a legitimate concern. But to encapsulate that spirit in the forms that we think we can carry over from the past is a will-o'-the-wisp endeavour beyond our power to command.

c. Lest the Corinthians imagine that the lack of some spectacular gift (tongues, healings, miracle-working) was a sign of divine disfavour the apostle reminds them that *the Spirit's sovereign disposing is the final rule*. In the statement of verse 11: 'It is one and the same Spirit who does all this; he gives a different gift to each person, as he wishes.' The last three words should sound the death-knell of all jealousy and envy as they surface in the church at Corinth (1 Cor. 4:6,7). In the following chapter (13:4) Paul writes a tribute to that love which 'is not jealous or conceited or proud.' Evidently the Corinthians were in fierce competition over the more remarkable phenomena in their church life. Paul has already had occasion to rebuke their pride (8:1,2). To counter their unbridled scrambling for what they deemed 'the best gifts' he lays down the principle that not all the gifts they considered important are indeed available. The rhetorical questions of 12:29,30 ('Are all apostles? . . . Do all work miracles? Do all possess gifts of healing? Do all speak with tongues?) each demands (in the Greek) the answer *No*. Not all Christians are intended to have these manifestations because not all these *charismata* are within the Spirit's good pleasure to bestow. Here is a further proof that what was said earlier about the limitation on the list in verses 8–10 is in accord with Paul's teaching.

d. The issue may well have been raised at Corinth: how can we place the gifts in their rightful priority? If the more 'showy' gifts are not approved – since the tendency to pride and self-importance as their accompaniment is only too obvious – which gifts are best?

Paul's counsel takes two lines. The unfailing criterion is *the promoting of the well-being of the entire community.* His term is 'upbuilding,' a word that runs like a thread through chapter 14 (verses 3,4,5,12,26). In chapter 12 the same insistence appears in verse 7: 'Each is given some proof of the Spirit's presence *for the good of all.*' Paul, here and elsewhere, is most anxious to have all gifts and graces serve one vital purpose – encouraging Christians to grow together by mutual support and strength.[6]

This goal can be attained only as each member is willing to subordinate his or her personal whims and wishes to the common good. So prophets must respect the claims of decorum and order (14:27–33,40); women must forgo abusing their gift and so disgracing the church's witness and their place in society[7] (14:34–36); tongues must be held in check if there is a likelihood that outsiders will only be confused by what they would regard as a cacophony (14:23). Paul's sensitivity in handling these matters is unmistakable: 'You must try above everything else to make greater use of those [gifts] which help to build up the church' (14:12).

The clinching appeal appears as the preface to his citation of the 'hymn of love' (ch. 13). 'Set your hearts, then, on the more important gifts' (12:31). But Paul does not do the expected thing, and go on to itemize these 'best gifts.' Instead he supplies a built-in corrective, as though to say: Whatever gift you may or may not have, be sure the exercise of that *charisma* is attended by, controlled by, and motivated by love. Lack of love will spoil even the most cherished gifts; absence of love will expose the flamboyant manifestations which pass for spiritual gifts; where love is missing, even sacrifice of one's life is in vain. In other words, Paul says, whatever is your spiritual asset, however weak, it is mighty if there is love. Where love is not present, outstanding gifts are misdirected and ephemeral.

5
Patterns of Ministry

The Church and Its Leaders

Right from the start of the church's existence as an organized community – however loosely structured we may judge it to have been – it has had leaders. Various historical factors contributed to this state of affairs, though to be sure the data may be interpreted in several ways.

Peter's Role

Those who insist that 'ministry' is as fundamental and necessary to the church's life and work as its existence and message will point to the so-called 'promise to Peter' (Matt. 16:19). There the pledge of Jesus is given: 'I will give you the keys of the kingdom of heaven; what you prohibit on earth will be prohibited in heaven and what you permit on earth will be permitted in heaven.' In the context of the confession just made by Peter at Caesarea Philippi, this is taken to be Jesus' reward and acknowledgement that 'on this rock foundation I will build my church' (Matt. 16:18). It follows that Peter was destined to become, and in fact did become, the link figure of early Christianity, uniting the heavenly Lord with the visible community of his people. Peter exercised the 'power of the keys' both at Pentecost and in Caesarea on the Mediterranean coast when he opened the door of faith to the family of the gentile Cornelius (Acts chs. 10,11). In the same role as intermediary he was seen at work in Samaria, conveying the power of the Spirit to new believers (Acts 8:14–25), and later acting as spokesman at the Jerusalem council in AD 49 (Acts 15).[1]

Whether in the interim between Acts 12:17 (where Peter, on his release from prison in Jerusalem, went off to another place) and Acts 15, he found his way back to Antioch (Gal. 2:11) and maybe to Rome is quite impossible to decide with any certainty. Much depends on the date of the Galatian epistle. Moreover the evidence for Peter's arrival in Rome in this period is meagre, and is almost certainly refuted by Paul's silence about Peter's presence in the imperial city prior to the writing of the letter to the Romans, about AD 57/58. It is more likely that Peter reached Corinth where he is known to have brought his wife on his missionary travels (1 Cor. 9:5) and where, possibly without his consent, a group arose naming itself after its allegiance to him (1 Cor. 1:12, 3:22).

The bones of this evidence are certainly sufficient to build up a skeletal figure of Peter as the early church leader whose presence was felt in the initial days of the Jerusalem church and beyond. But whether the evidence says more than this is open to question, and we may simply raise the issues that present themselves.

a. Exactly what is implied in the 'promise to Peter' and the exercise of his authority? We note the Jewish character of the language and its symbolism. The parallels in the judgment passed by Jesus on the religious leaders who were confronting the Matthean church (Matt. 23:13) suggest a polemical thrust in Matthew 16:19. The terms used both in 16:19 and 18:18 (cf. John 20:23) have heavy judicial overtones.

Thus it appears that Peter and his fellow-apostles have power to dispense the word of grace and judgment in the assurance that the risen Lord will uphold their decisions in his name.[2] The stories in the early parts of Acts show them doing exactly that by inviting men and women to enter the gate of the kingdom and by passing sentence on impenitent sinners (Acts 5:1–11, 8:20–24). Yet the authority is derivative in both instances, since Peter can neither confer forgiveness – he can and does simply confirm it (Acts 2:38, 3:19) – nor is it his prerogative to execute judgment. That solemn work is in higher hands (Acts 5:4,9, 8:21). Acts 3:6, 'I will give you what I have: in the name of Jesus Christ of Nazareth I order you to walk!' neatly sums up his opportunity and responsibility. But nothing more.

b. Peter's disappearance from the scene at Acts 12:17 is mysterious. Evidently the notice is supplied to inform the reader that Peter escaped from the place of danger. Therefore he must have left Jerusalem. But where he went off to is anybody's guess. As we observed, the odds are against a visit to Rome, unless Paul's veiled allusion in Romans 15:20 ('the foundation laid by *someone else*') refers to Peter. But this idea is speculative.

c. The visit to Antioch led to a showdown since it brought Peter and Paul into open dispute (see Gal. 2:11–14). The disagreement centred on the conditions by which table fellowship between Jewish believers and Gentile Christians was to be made possible. Peter at first adopted an accommodating line, following his own experience of the revelation that came to him at Joppa (Acts 10:9–16). But under Judaizing pressure he pulled away and 'played the Pharisee' (Gal. 2:12) by separating himself from the brethren and refusing to eat with those who had not accepted Jewish circumcision as Christians. Paul saw the danger (verse 14), and publicly rebuked him 'because he was clearly wrong' (verse 11). Happily Peter profited from this confrontation, if we are correct in placing the Jerusalem council meeting somewhat later in time. Then he came out boldly with as succinct a statement of the 'gospel according to Paul' as Paul himself was ever likely to frame (Acts 15:11). But the interesting side-light is how Peter's apostolic authority could be successfully resisted, his behaviour and decisions shown to be lamentable when tested in public debate, and his standing rehabilitated only as he returned to 'the truth of the gospel' (Gal. 2:14), as Paul understood it.

d. In all the data relating to Petrine authority there is no hint that importance is attached to his personal stature, although it may be granted that the best understanding of the promise, 'You are a rock, Peter, and on this rock I will build my church' (Matt. 16:18), is in terms of Peter's person as the original witness and confessor of the messianic faith. Certainly the foundation laid by the apostolic witness in Ephesians 2:20; Revelation 21:14 is a once-for-all task and need not be repeated. To that extent the promise to Peter is 'limited to a specific lifetime. In other words, the task which Peter is given to fulfil is unique, and this makes possible the building of the Church.'[3] Any notion of a transferred authority extending across succeeding generations is not to be found in this passage. Peter's own role is seen in 1 Peter 5:1–5 where his testament is given: and that is in the language of his privilege as leader and eyewitness who set the good example to those who were to follow. The 'apostolic authority' is thought of in those terms, and none other.

Corinthian House-groups

At the opposite end of the spectrum a view that takes its point of departure from the descriptions in 1 Corinthians portrays this early church's life and structure as quite loose, flexible and amorphous.[4] In a context such as that given in 1 Corinthians 14:26 the congregation meets for corporate worship with a minimum of organization and control. No one person evidently is in charge. 'Each person' makes his or her own contribution whether in the form of a hymn, a teaching, a revelation from God, a 'message with a strange sound' (=glossolalia), and its accompanying explanation.

Paul sees the obvious dangers inherent in this situation, and his surrounding discussion is aimed at supplying some ways of checking excess and promoting good order (1 Cor. 14:23–25,40). He knows that there are prophets who aspire to leadership, and he summons them to obey his directives. There are those who were styled 'spiritual people' (14:37; compare Gal. 6:1), and they too are called to be accountable. But at first glance the atmosphere at church gatherings at Corinth appears such as to highlight the spontaneous nature of the proceedings, and traces of ministerial order seem remote.

Yet there are counterbalancing data, which may be listed briefly.

a. Some of the leaders at Corinth are explicitly named. 'Stephanas and his family' (1 Cor. 1:16, 16:15) have given themselves to the service of the church. Paul is not reluctant to appeal to his readers 'to follow the leadership of such people as these, and of anyone else who works and serves with them' (16:16).[5] The translation just given is decidedly weak; Paul is in fact urging the Corinthians to 'be subject to such persons' in Stephanas' household who have taken on themselves the responsibility of *diakonia* or ministry. These leaders seem to have some specific role in the congregation which has duly authorized them to act, and Paul for that reason is not slow to call for submission to their authority in a way parallel with 1 Thessalonians 5:12 (a verse that incidentally uses the same verb for service, rendered 'work,' *kopiaō*, as in 1 Cor. 16:16).

b. 1 Corinthians 11:19 also refers (although obliquely) to leaders at Corinth. Whether Paul is speaking playfully or ironically or derisively is not clear. He singles out 'those who are approved among you' (*hoi dokimoi en hymin*) and comments that one result of the divisions plaguing this community was that these persons were brought to the fore. 'It had to be,' he concludes. Maybe these folk are no better than party ringleaders and spokespersons for the Apollos-group or the Peter-party; Paul can hardly have viewed the scene with pleasure, especially as his own name was involved as well. But it does still appear that this was the leadership at Corinth, however much perverted and sadly off-course it was. Here is a further objection to regarding the Corinthian church as a structure-less assembly, with nobody guiding it.

c. The clearest example in 1 Corinthians of Paul's intention to describe a church with a regular ministry comes in 12:27–30. While reaffirming that all the believers share a place in the body of Christ as integral members, Paul insists that not all are intended to be in positions of leadership.

'In the church, then, God has put all in place: in the first place apostles, in the second place prophets, and in the third place teachers. . . . They are not all apostles or prophets or teachers.'

The major titles are listed in order of priority. 'Apostles' formed the original core or nucleus of witness to the historical events that lay at the heart of the church's preaching. An important qualification that restricted membership to the company called 'apostles' in the narrower sense is provided in Acts 1:21,22. There the successor to the recently deceased Judas Iscariot is selected according to stated criteria: 'Someone must join us as a witness to the resurrection of the Lord Jesus. He must be one of the men who were in our group during the whole time that the Lord Jesus travelled about with us.' The successful candidate was Matthias who took 'this place of service as an apostle' (1:25). Interestingly, no attempt was made to bring this number of twelve up to strength when it was again depleted at the martyrdom of James, the brother of John (Acts 12:2). Perhaps we are to infer that the 'Twelve' was a technical term – as in 1 Corinthians 15:5 – and that once the work of the apostles had been performed, their number could be permitted to diminish according to the natural consequences of death and disappearance from the scene.

The work to be done by the apostles is spelled out in Ephesians 2:20: the church is built upon the foundation representing or laid by the apostles and prophets, the cornerstone being Christ Jesus himself (compare Rev. 21:14: the names of the twelve apostles are inscribed on the foundation stones of the heavenly city of God).

'Apostleship' carries a wider range of meaning when it is thought of as attaching to persons like Epaphroditus (Phil. 2:25: 'Your messenger,' Greek *apostolos*) and probably Andronicus and Junias who 'are well known among the apostles' (Rom. 16:7 – or as it may be translated, 'well known *as* apostles'). In the more restricted sense it applies to those persons to whom it was granted to see the exalted Christ and to be commissioned by him as eyewitness. In addition to the Twelve James (1 Cor. 15:7; Gal. 1:19, 2:9) is probably to be reckoned in this group; and Paul too claimed a place by virtue of his having seen the risen Lord (1 Cor. 9:1: Am I not an apostle? Haven't I seen Jesus our Lord?) and having been set apart for this service at his behest (Rom. 1:1; Gal. 1:1). To Paul the 'secret,' the news of the inclusion of Gentile believers in the one body of the church, was given by divine revelation in the Spirit. It is exactly this gospel which for Paul constituted the essence of his apostolic calling (Gal. 2:7; Rom. 15:16; cf. Eph. 3:5,6). It cannot be accidental that Paul is called 'apostle' (Acts 14:4,14) in connection with his first missionary outreach to uncircumcized Gentiles, since he and his party had been 'sent out' (literally 'made apostles') by the Spirit, in Acts 13:2,3.

In the Corinthian list 'prophets' go closely with 'apostles'; and the two offices are linked to the point of identity in Ephesians 2:20, 3:5.[6] The prophets are the leaders and speakers of the new age who announce the coming of God's saviour and with him the arrival of a new chapter in God's dealings with men and women.

New Testament Models of Ministry

a. We are led to the conclusion that, as far as the churches of Paul's apostolic foundation were concerned, some type of regular leadership was formed right from the beginning. The reference in 1 Thessalonians 5:12,13 has already been mentioned. In more specific terms the leaders at Philippi are greeted by their title, 'bishops (RSV marg. overseers) and deacons' (Phil. 1:1). The terms here apparently describe the tasks these people were called to undertake.[7] The *episkopoi* as the name suggests were to be 'shepherds' protecting and nourishing the flock, exactly as defined in Acts 20:28 where RSV employs the translation 'guardians' for the same Greek term. Most interpreters see an equivalence between this function and that implied in the name given to the leaders whom Paul is addressing at Miletus, according to the Acts record (Acts 20:17). They are 'elders' appointed by the church, evidently after the pattern of the Jewish synagogue which had *zeqenim* or 'elders' as its leaders.

The Philippian 'deacons' are simply 'servants' (*diakonoi*) charged with some special responsibility in the congregation; this may or may not be linked with the love-gift the Philippian church had sent to Paul through Epaphroditus' mission

(4:18). If it is, there is an appropriateness about Paul's placing the names of these men at the head of the letter, especially as 1:3 may well veil an allusion to his thanks to God 'for all their remembrance of him' (see Moffatt) in his need. On this basis, we could distinguish the assignments of 'overseer' and 'deacon' as concerned respectively with spiritual ministrations and financial responsibilities.

Yet no clear demarcation was made in the early church as we observe from the appointment of the 'seven' (Acts 6). These hellenist Christians were chosen to 'handle finances' (6:2), particularly in regard to the distribution of funds to needy widows in the congregation. The men so elected were known for their spiritual capacities (6:3) more than for their business acumen. And of the seven names in 6:5, at least two – Philip and Stephen – employed their gifts in a preaching ministry. Their being 'set apart' by the apostles and/or the assembly (the text is not clear in Acts 6:6) is a further token of the need for 'order' in the embryonic church. Luke has also placed on record the appointment of 'elders' in churches established in Asia Minor as a result of Paul's first Gentile mission (Acts 14:23). We are safe in concluding that Paul's church planting work included the setting up of a rudimentary organization that may be designated 'pastors and deacons.' Women deacons also are mentioned, with at least one person, Phoebe, named (Rom. 16:1).

b. At Jerusalem there was a different model of leadership. As we have seen, the chief figure was Peter who played the leading and speaking part in the first scenes of the primitive church's decision-making and witness. He is often mentioned as accompanied by John (Acts 3:1, 4:13, 8:14). However John (presumably the son of Zebedee) serves only in a minor, non-speaking capacity, and sometimes appears as a 'lay' figure in the scenario.

Peter's disappearance after his release from prison (Acts 12:17) presents a further strange part of the story. Peter acknowledges that in his absence his place has been taken by James, the Lord's brother; hence the report is naturally to be taken to James (Acts 12:17: 'Tell this to James and the rest of the [?his] brothers'). It is a likely guess that James, won over to the messianic belief by a personal resurrection-appearance (1 Cor. 15:7; contrast John 7:5), was given a place of pre-eminence in the Jerusalem church on account of his representing the holy family who became identified with the messianic movement from the beginning (Acts 1:14). If James is rightly called an 'apostle' – and this depends on how Galatians 1:19 is read – it is then not difficult to understand how he would be accorded such honour in the church. He had seen the risen Lord, and so he met at least one of the qualifications listed in Acts 1:22. He presided at the apostolic conference in Acts 15 and gave a decisive ruling (Acts 15:13–21), though the edict is sent out in the name of 'the apostles and the elders' who comprised the collegial leadership of the Jerusalem mother church. Perhaps most significantly, when Paul returned to Jerusalem from ministry in the Gentile churches, it was to James he reported (Acts 21:17–19). There James acted as a presiding bishop surrounded by a college of elders; and they prescribed for Paul what needed to be done to avert criticism of his Gentile ministry. James is firmly in the seat of authority; and it is left to the early gnostic literature to magnify his status beyond all recognition. For example in the gnostic *Gospel of Thomas* (saying 12), Jesus predicts James' rank in a sort of caliphate: asked about who will take over when he has gone, Jesus responds, 'You will go to James the just, for whose sake heaven and earth were made.'

c. A third specimen of ministerial oversight appears in Acts 13:1–3, describing the church at Antioch in Syria. 'There were [*some* – not in Greek] prophets and teachers,' whose names are listed beginning with Barnabas and concluding with Saul. The activity of these men is evidently related to what follows: 'While they were serving (worshipping, RSV) the Lord and fasting . . . .' Life in the incipient community at Antioch, the third city of the Roman empire after Rome and Alexandria in Egypt, had earlier been described in Acts 11:19–26. The Gentile mission here got under way in earnest and with great success. The need for teachers was not surprising; and it was in that capacity that Saul of Tarsus was brought from his native city to assist in the work. He and

Barnabas 'met with the people of the church and taught a large group.' The twofold ministry of 'prophets' and 'teachers' is in line with the situation as we have described.

In this context 'prophets' are to be understood as proclaimers of the word (Acts 11:20: 'preaching the Good News about the Lord Jesus, or "Jesus as Lord" '). This is in contrast to the prophetic task of Agabus who is introduced in the next section with an obvious change of meaning. Agabus predicted the great famine that was to occur in Claudius' reign, AD 46–48; and he exercised a similar predictive ministry in a later meeting with Paul (Acts 21:10,11: at Caesarea Agabus on a visit from Jerusalem foretold the warning of Paul's arrest in the holy city). The prophets mentioned in Acts 13:1 are more of the type whose work is described in 1 Corinthians 11:4,5, 14:3 where the text neatly sums up the vocation and scope of the prophet's ministry: 'one who speaks God's message (Greek *prophēteuein*) speaks to men, and gives them help, encouragement, and comfort.'[8] But here too there is an evangelistic edge to this ministry of the spoken word, as is clear from 1 Corinthians 14:24. When God's message is 'prophesied,' not only are believers established (verse 22); some unbeliever or outsider, if he is drawn in to the assembly, will be convinced of his sin by what he hears and led to confession and worship (verse 25). This result indicates the 'charismatic' power of the prophet no less than the obvious pneumatic work of Agabus.

'Teachers' perform the role of instruction required once the evangelist has presented the saving message. There is a logical sequence in the lists given in 1 Corinthians 12:28,29 and Ephesians 4:11 as well as Acts 13:1. Teachers are required to be 'men of the spirit' and have a God-appointed rank, but their function seems to be a ministry that is 'non-pneumatic'; they 'edify the congregation by means of their own clearer understanding.'[9] The quality of life exhibited by the teachers is to be in keeping with the content of what they teach. Hence the pointed warnings in James 3:1 and the example of Jezebel 'a prophetess': she teaches and 'misleads my servants into committing immorality' (Rev. 2:20). In the *Didache*, a church order representing 'The Teaching of the Apostles' and dated between AD 80–100, the quality of life shown by the itinerant prophet, whether he stays too long in one place or asks for money for himself, is offered as a criterion to test his genuineness.[10]

Diversity-in-unity

So far we have covered the main items of evidence concerning 'ministry' in the various centres of first (and later) generation Christianity. According to the geographical areas the offices of leadership are called by different titles and imply different functions.[11]

a. In the mother church in Jerusalem, the early primacy of Peter is replaced by an 'episcopate' of James who is surrounded by a college of elders. He acts as a presiding elder, but with a clear aura of personal authority, probably attributed to his family connection with Jesus his brother 'according to natural descent.'

b. At Antioch in Syria more of a 'presbyterial' arrangement prevails, with 'prophets and teachers' forming a consortium of leadership. These men may have received a roving commission which took them to other mission centres, as Paul and Barnabas evidently did and as seems to be the case in the *Didache* or Teaching of the Twelve Apostles.

c. In the Pauline churches, established by Paul's own work as 'apostle to the Gentiles' following the concordat of Galatians 2:7,8, 'elders' were appointed, though they are otherwise referred to as 'those who are over you in the Lord' (1 Thess. 5:12), or 'your leaders' (Heb. 13:17) in churches not of Paul's founding. Paul claimed authority to be 'an expert builder' (1 Cor. 3:10) and to lay a firm foundation (1 Cor. 3:10; Rom. 15:20), though this claim was not uncontested in spite of his appeal to divine authorization (Gal. 1:11–24). The rise and influence of 'false apostles' (2 Cor. 11:13) at Corinth and probably elsewhere (for instance at Thessalonica and Philippi) threw him on to the defensive, and he had repeatedly to clarify the meaning of 'true'[12] apostolic service over against what he regarded as a woeful misconception in terms of lordly power, exhibitionism and unscrupulous domineering of the various congregations (see 2 Cor. chs. 10–13). The need for wise leadership was never more obviously felt than at Corinth where self-centred individualism and unconcern for the lowly fellow-believer had got quite out of hand.

d. Already in the Johannine church circles the same unseemly aspirations to ecclesiastical power were evident. The 'deceivers' in the congregation were bent on opposing the Elder's authority (1 John 2:26,27) and prophets who claimed to teach an understanding of the person of Christ at variance with John's teaching are unmasked as 'false' (1 John 4:1–6; 2 John 7–9). In the third letter John has to deal with the case of Diotrephes, a demagogic ecclesiastical statesman who is maligning his position as an exponent of 'the truth' (3 John 9,10).

e. Provision for the days of the church's future development is the theme of the so-called Pastoral letters. They envisage the church as an institutional body,[13] moving into a period of settling down in contemporary society, as the prospect of an immediate return of the Lord in glory begins to fade, false teaching on the horizon requires a firm rebuttal, and the question of a succession of leadership is a pressing concern. All these matters form the background of these letters, which are traditionally ascribed to Paul and may well contain the germ or outline of what he had in mind for the consolidation of the work in centres such as Ephesus where Timothy is a kind of 'diocesan bishop' (1 Tim. 1:3) and Crete to whose care Titus has been appointed (Tit. 1:5). These precious letters set the stage for the way Christians in a later generation sought to apply the apostle's teaching in areas which included the proper ordering of divine worship (1 Tim. 2:1–15), the treatment of widows (1 Tim. 5:1–16), and the suitable safeguards of delegated responsibilities shared among 'overseers' (1 Tim. 3:1–7; Tit. 1:5–9 where 'elders' and 'bishops' are two names for the same office), deacons (1 Tim. 3:8–10,12,13) and deaconesses (1 Tim. 3:9). Timothy's own office is highly regarded (1 Tim. 1:18, 4:14; 2 Tim. 1:6,7), yet he must apply himself to his work with all diligence so that his ministerial example will be blameless (1 Tim. 4:11–16; 2 Tim. 2:15) as Paul himself has always striven to set an exemplary pattern (2 Tim. 3:10–14).

One verse perhaps sums up the ethos of the Pastoral epistles. 'Take the words that you heard me preach in the presence of many witnesses, and give them into the keeping of men you can trust, men who will be able to teach others also' (2 Tim. 2:2). The 'faithful men' who are required to keep alive the apostolic deposit of gospel truth as Paul had entrusted it to Timothy (2 Tim. 1:12–14) will ensure the continuance of ministry. In a document known as First Clement, to be dated AD 96, written from Rome to Corinth, the same prescriptions are found (ch. 44).

The line of development, necessary to maintain and ensure a 'succession' of duly appointed ministerial offices in the church, runs on to a fully articulated system of hierarchical control in the time of Ignatius, bishop of Antioch in the first decade of the second century. For Ignatius the bishop is the necessary link between the heavenly Lord and his people on earth, and baptisms and the Lord's supper services are not 'valid' unless the bishop presides or authorizes them. We have travelled a long way from the free spontaneity of church gatherings at Corinth in the middle 50s of the first century. Yet the ground has been prepared for this development, partly by historical pressures such as the need to have a 'presiding elder' at the table of the Lord. This person became the church's spokesman in civic affairs as the church grew in strength and social importance in the community. Preparation was also made by the church's own evolving self-consciousness as a corporate entity, and the need to regulate its worshipping life was increasingly felt.

f. This period of the church's 'adjustment to world-history,' as it has been called,[14] is characterized by several diverse features. The passing of the apostolic generation as its notable leaders were taken from the scene, a coming to grips with the phenomenon of physical growth, both in numbers and in a territorial sense as the Christian mission reached out across the Mediterranean world from its home-base in the Syrian Levant, and the call to withstand opposition from the Roman state which was forced to take recognition of the social effects of this expanding religious movement – these are perhaps the chief signs that prompted the framing of a clearly defined 'doctrine of ministry.' We turn now to consider such a statement of ministry in the post-Pauline period, though there are clear lines of development from the apostle's teaching.

The Witness of Ephesians

One New Testament document in particular looks toward future development: *the epistle to the Ephesians*. Debate over the setting of this document in the Pauline 'library' is still going on. Some interpreters regard it as the crown of the apostle's teaching deepened and enlarged during his final days of imprisonment at Rome. Others argue that it represents an extension and fresh application of Paul's understanding of the church to a situation that arose only after his death. Either way, it contains the fullest expression in the New Testament scriptures of how Christians will increasingly come to view the universal church and its patterns of ministry. In Ephesians the church takes on a cosmic significance as 'the completion of him (Christ the exalted Lord) who himself completes all things everywhere' (1:23) and is described as already glorified with a glory that belongs properly to the age to come (2:6, 3:21, 5:26,27 – three churchly texts that mark a considerable advance on the teaching we have considered up to this point: they stand in contrast to the idea of a church struggling in this world and awaiting its eternal reward in the next life). Not surprisingly the prospect of the Lord's coming for the church at his advent is replaced by the thought of the church at present exalted with the risen Christ. The church has its life stretching before it on earth to an unknown future because it shares now the life of its heavenly Lord.

Two important corollaries follow in regard to the church's self-understanding; both have a distinct bearing on the ministry. One is that the teaching on the church as Christ's body, found in Romans 12:4,5 and 1 Corinthians 12:12–27, has undergone a decisive developmental change. In the earlier

Pauline descriptions the church was likened to a body on the analogy of the human frame which has many parts as limbs and sinews but remains 'one body.' In Ephesians the unity of the church is an article of faith and Christ's having a body is a necessity to understanding and fulfilling his mission in God's cosmic plan. The teaching begins with the assertion in 1:10: 'God's plan . . . is to bring all creation together . . . with *Christ as head*.' The microcosm of this universe which will one day eventuate from God's design and its execution is the church, with which Christ as head is indissolubly linked (1:22,23) since the church 'complements' him; and either Christ-without-the-church or the church-without-Christ is as monstrous a thought as a bodiless head or a headless body! So from the earlier apostolic description of the church = the body of Christ in a figurative or metaphorical way – 'the church is *like* the body of Christ' – in Ephesians the equation speaks more of a metaphysical or substantive character. 'The church *is* his body' as being needful to express his fulness and the completion of God's saving plan for the broken world. The same conclusion stands at the end of the discussion in Ephesians 5:25–33 where husband and wife are inextricably linked in God's creation-will as 'one flesh' (Gen. 2:24); and the comment is appended, 'I understand it [this scripture] as applying to Christ and the church' (5:32) since he is the preserver of his body, the church (5:23).

The other consequence follows immediately. Given the transcendental nature of the church's life, even in this present world which is yet a place of conflict, though the real engagement is supra-terrestrial (6:12), it is not such a long step to confess the church as one of the articles of belief. 'I believe in . . . one holy catholic apostolic church' comes easily to the lips of the modern Christian, but it is worth pointing out that this is an audacious claim when it is set alongside the earlier statements: 'I believe in God the Father Almighty . . . and in Jesus Christ his only Son our Lord . . . the Holy Ghost.' This step has been taken in Ephesians in a way quite unparalleled in other New Testament writings. Ephesians 4:4–6 uses a rudimentary credal formulary to express just that belief, employing a veiled trinitarian idiom but affirming that 'there is one body.' The church itself is included within all that the confessing community attests!

The previous discussion – if it is on the right track – is necessary to pave the way for a look at Ephesians 4:7–16. To fasten on the main item in this intricate passage will be enough to lead to a conclusion that will round off the chapter.

Christ's gifts to his church are those who fulfil the leadership offices referred to in verse 11. They are given 'to prepare all God's people for the work of Christian service in order to build up the body of Christ' (verse 12). The question is, how do they do it?

A recent simple answer is that the ministers 'equip the saints,' the laity, by elevating them as a group to their level and so democratizing the concept of ministry. The slogan is then coined: all God's people are ministers, and the 'ordained' branch functions simply as enablers or facilitators to permit and encourage the rank-and-file believer to discover and perform his or her 'ministry.'

This is an appealing idea, to be sure; and it fits easily into the modern world-view of equality and a 'we're-all-in-it-together' mentality. But it hardly squares with the exegesis of verses 15, 16. There once more we meet Christ as the body's head. He controls the different parts of his body (=his people) and sees to it that they fit together into a harmonious whole. We can now add the middle term in the equation: Christ the head = his body, the church. It is through 'every joint' (or ligament or connection)[15] that the whole body is compacted and unified; and each part is supplied with a connecting joint. The link with verses 11, 12 is clear. The heavenly Lord works to control, to unify, to use the various parts of his body through his gifts of ministers. It is they who act as Christ's messengers to direct the body, and so prepare all God's people to engage in his service. In the upbuilding of the body – 'upbuilding and body are interchangeable terms' as Vielhauer reminds us [16] – which comes about through 'each separate part working as it should,' the intermediary 'joints' play a vital role in the analogy. This may appear at first glance a mechanistic outworking: Christ→his ministers→the church. The church thus seems to depend on the ministry. But this conclusion is tempered by (*a*) the reminder that the ministers are themselves Christ's gift to the church, not authority figures in their own right, (*b*) the caution that they also are 'under his control' (verse 16) and are themselves part of the body, not separate from it, and (*c*) the wording of verse 16*d*: the 'the whole body grows and builds itself up *through love*.'

Conclusion

We are led to conclude that 'patterns of ministry' mean different things at changing times and are adapted to local needs. The needful place of ministry, whether 'ordained' or not, is clear, since God fulfils his purpose in many directions and in ways that *may* be unpredictable yet are usually known by what he has revealed in his word and in the life and experience of the early church. If this is not so and we may expect God to break out in fresh revelation anywhere, what becomes of our confidence in the normative control of scripture over the church?

Finally, it should be obvious that no one pattern of ministry can claim to be exclusive and binding on all Christians in every place for all time.[17] The deciding criterion has to be 'what is good for the church,' its *bene esse*, and will thereby promote its true life in Christ and serve its mission to be Christ's visible presence in the world of our day and all the days to come.

Additional Note

Comment on Ephesians 2:20

The most comprehensive discussion of this verse I know of is J. Pfammatter, *Die Kirche als Bau*. Eine exegetisch-theologische Studie zur Ekklesiologie der Paulusbriefe (Analecta Gregoriana, Rome, 1960) pp. 78–97.

His conclusions, with some of the evidence, may be summarized here, since they offer a novel interpretation not usually considered.

The deceptively simple phrase 'the foundation of the

apostles and prophets' yields no fewer than three possibilities of meaning of the genitive:

1. possession. The foundation on which the church is erected is that on which the apostles and prophets themselves rest. Anselm and Aquinas held this view.

2. origin. The foundation is that laid by the apostles and prophets – a view that goes back to Ambrosiaster and is championed by some older Protestant commentators. Cf. NEB, *Good News Bible*.

3. explanation or apposition. The foundation consists of the apostles and prophets. Found in Chrysostom and Theophylact, this understanding is shared by many modern scholars, e.g. Dibelius, Abbott, Benoit (in the Jerusalem Bible), Schlier and K. L. Schmidt, *TDNT* 3, p. 63, as well as Pfammatter himself who notes that interpretations *1.* and *2.* are motivated by a desire to harmonize Ephes. 2:20 with 1 Cor. 3:11 where the foundation is Christ himself. But the effort breaks down on the observation that in Ephesians Christ is the cornerstone different from the foundation.

But there is no great disparity between the *ultimate* meaning of *2.* and *3.* It is difficult to separate Christ as the true foundation from those who proclaim him, as E. Best notes: 'If Apostles . . . were those who laid foundations [cf. 1 Cor. 3:10; Rom. 15:20], it is a probable association of ideas to think of them as themselves the foundation stones' (*One Body in Christ*, 1955, p. 164).

In other words, it is the *proclaimed Christ* who is the basis of the new temple; and in that activity of preaching the apostles and prophets play a unique role because it is their ministry in the apostolate that lays the foundation. Not that they are the foundation in their persons but rather in the exercise of their function as official bearers of the revelation of Christ (so J. Murphy-O'Connor, *Paul on Preaching*, 1964, p. 286). H. Schlier may be quoted (*Der Brief an die Epheser*, 1957, p. 142):

The 'preached' Christ cannot be separated from the apostle and his apostolate. There is no access to Christ other than through the apostles and prophets, who have preached him and who themselves become and remain in their preaching the foundation.

If we understand 'apostles and prophets' to include both their oral witness and their literary deposits in the New Testament scriptures, this is exactly a statement of Reformed teaching on *sola scriptura* which 'drives' us to Christ.

Underlying Pfammatter's exposition are two other issues deftly handled in his treatment. One is a report on the growing consensus of opinion that in Ephesians 2:20 'prophets' means New Testament prophets as in the parallel verses of this epistle (3:5, 4:11); and the order 'apostles and prophets' confirms this, making it difficult to suppose that Old Testament prophets would be placed in second rank. But are these 'prophets' comparable with the men of Acts 13:1, 15:22,32 or 11:27,28 = 21:10 (Agabus), or the women of Acts 21:9 (the daughters of Philip)? Or is the text referring to the charismatics of 1 Cor. 11 and 14?

The second part of Pfammatter's discussion picks up a hint dropped by P. Joüon, 'Notes de philologie paulinienne,' *Recherches de science religieuse* 15, 1925, pp. 532–34, who observes the single definite article before 'apostles' which then governs the second noun in the pair (as in 1 Cor. 15:24; Eph. 5:20 as well as Tit. 2:13). This linguistic feature suggests that one entity, not two, is in view, and that we should regard 'apostles' and 'prophets' as referring to the same persons under two guises. 'Apostles' speaks of their mission, 'prophets' indicates the way by which they exercise that mission in announcing God's word – so Joüon, p. 533, who helpfully quotes Romans 1:1. Paul is 'an apostle of Jesus Christ' *and* 'set apart for the gospel' as prophet. He is both apostle and prophet in one person unlike the persons whose description in 4:11 suggests two separate offices.

The conclusion is that in Ephesians there are not two groups that constitute the church's foundation, but one: apostle-prophets. To them is given the privilege of an authorized commission and of representing Christ and witnessing to the mystery (3:5) as 'original apostles' (*Urapostel*) who like the Twelve and Paul play a unique role: they also as prophets convey authentic teaching and preaching – a work

that apparently links them with others yet is treated as unique
in 1 Tim. 2:7; 2 Tim. 1:11. But only this select band combines
in one person this double function. Others may be 'apostles'
(such as Barnabas or maybe James the Lord's brother or the
'pillars' of Gal. 2:9); others may exercise the charismatic
ministry of 'prophecy' in a line stretching from Anna (Luke
2:36) to John's Apocalypse (Rev. 22:6–10). From the perspective of what is written in Ephesians the Pauline apostolate
alone qualifies for a description that marks it out as unique
in the history of salvation (called 'insight into the mystery'
of 'one holy catholic apostolic' church [Pfammatter's heading, p. 73]). It is this group of 'apostle-prophets' chiefly
represented by Paul the great exponent of a united church,
'one new man,' that is dignified with the epithet 'holy' (3:5)
and held up to veneration as part of a fervent call of obedience
to Paul's gospel.

If this conclusion fails to convince, especially when the
purpose of Ephesians is under debate, at least the proposal
of an order of 'apostle-prophets,' suggested by Joüon, Pfammatter and Murphy-O'Connor, does contribute to a clearer
understanding of how flexibly the term 'apostle' is used – as
L. Cerfaux, 'Pour l'histoire du titre "Apostolos" dans le
NT,' *Recherches de science religieuse* 48, 1960, pp. 76–92,
has shown – and adds in a third category to supplement the
customary twofold distinction (i.e. original followers of Jesus
in Acts 1, and representatives or delegates like Epaphroditus
whose work is patterned on the Jewish model of *shaliach*.
The latter was a messenger sent from his principal, especially
from the synagogues of the Dispersion, to fulfil a
commission).

6
Understanding the Ordinances: Symbols or Sacraments?

The Means of Grace

The central teaching of the New Testament about the relationship between Christ and the church is that he 'has authority over the church' (Eph. 5:23). The language used in the Ephesian epistle underscores that idea: Christ has a *body* (1:23, 4:4, 5:23) of which he is head; Christ erects and owns a *building* (2:21,22) of which he is both foundation and the strength of its growth; and Christ claims a *bride* (5:25–33) of which he is the loving, caring, providing, yet controlling spouse.[1]

Dominating all these images is the thought of Christ's firm control of his people. His rightful name is 'Lord' which has the same connotation, 'lordship' implying ownership and the power to command.

How is it possible for the heavenly, unseen Lord to make his will and plan known to his people on earth? In considering their openness to his pressure we note the practice and discipline of prayer, both in private and in public worship. Prayer as a means of communion and communication between the head of the church and its scattered members has always been highly regarded, even if Christians have often paid lip-service to prayer rather than practise it.

In considering the channels of communication by means of which the church's Lord comes to his people in every age, we are led to examine the scope and significance of what are traditionally known as 'the means of grace.' These are the appointed or experienced modes in which Christ Jesus intimates his presence and makes known his mind to his church for its direction and good.

a. An important tradition places emphasis on the ministry of the word as a vehicle of revelation and grace: it is *the preaching of the gospel* that is chiefly regarded as 'effective.' The logical flow of Paul's thought in Romans 10:14,15 originates in the question, If men need to invoke the Lord's name (=his self-revelation) to find salvation, how can they do this? This 'calling on his name' has behind it the exercise of faith which in turn presupposes their hearing the message. Yet, 'How can they hear, if the message is not preached? And how can the message be preached, if the messengers are not sent out?' Paul ends with an Old Testament testimony to validate the commissioning of preachers (in Isa. 52:7) just as he began with a scriptural citation from Joel 2:23 in verse 13. His argument runs from the present enjoyment of new life in Christ back through the human response in faith to where it begins, in the 'preaching about Christ' (Rom. 10:17).

The value Paul set on preaching is clear; he sees it as the essential link between the mystery of the gospel and its being understood and received by men and women. Moreover it is along this avenue that the living Christ comes to his church in all ages; in that respect preaching is a conveyance of his grace. The proclamation of God's word in Christ assumes a word-of-God character as it is faithfully preached and savingly believed. This is the implication of his statement in 2 Corinthians 5:20: 'Here we are, then, speaking for Christ, as though God himself were appealing to you through us.'[2]

b. The dimension of public worship has always been understood as revelation, since it provides a rare 'moment' or 'occasion' (Greek *kairos*) when God's grace and human aspiration, need and resolve intersect in time. The story of Jacob's ladder in Genesis 28:10–17 may be taken (as in John 1:51) as a picture of this two-way traffic. God's angels ascending and descending represent the intercourse between earth and heaven. Human desires and designs are lifted up to God's presence; his mercy, favour and help are pledged in response to man's need.

But more than that, Jacob's vision was evidently that of 'a stairway . . . set on the ground, with its top reaching to the sky' (E. A. Speiser's rendering of verse 12).[3] This imagery accounts for Jacob's later description of the heavenly ramp as a 'gateway to heaven' (verse 17) – to the very abode of deity. In other words God was himself in touch with the patriarch to assure him of his presence in the present (verse 16). In that 'moment' of worship, symbolized by Jacob's setting up a stone pillar and consecrating it with oil, God came to this man and he responded. Local colour and contemporary imagery (drawn from Mesopotamian ziggurats discovered at Ur) blend in with the innate human need in the story to seek contact with God who in turn is graciously pleased to reveal himself through tangible and visible tokens. The essence of Christian worship, enriched indeed by the fuller understanding of God that we have in Christ and by the Spirit, is compacted into this single 'old world' tale. And John's gospel seizes upon it to enforce the point, which will be further elaborated at John 4:21–24.

c. Awareness of the divine presence does not always wait on our preparing for it or striving to achieve it. This contention is clear in the parable of Matthew 25:31–46. *The service of those in distress* is an avenue along which Christ comes to his people today; even when they seem ostensibly to be involved in an activity that is 'non-religious.' But at a deeper level the issues have to do with support of and help to missionaries in distress, and so relate to an identity with Christ's cause in the world, not general philanthropy. What counts is true motive. 'These brothers of mine' in their need are those who have endured hardship and privation out of loyalty to Christ;[4] the group standing at the king's right hand side are the sensitive and caring church who reach out the helping hand simply to aid them. To their surprise Christ is one with his afflicted people – as in Acts 9:4; 1 Corinthians 8:12 – and he is there in all acts of compassionate and loving and costly ministration offered in his name. The cup of water, proffered in that name, becomes sacramental as it conveys and realizes his presence and grace (Matt. 10:42). Obedient followers who are alive to human need wherever (but particularly as it concerns the household of faith) it may be found and who attempt to meet it as his people find that they come to know their Lord in fresh ways as they do his will in daily life and duty (John 7:17).

d. Two other 'occasions' of divine self-revealing have been observed in the church since its inception; and they are normally thought of in the phrase 'means of grace.' *Baptism and the Lord's Supper* are treasured and practised as rites that carry the hallmark of Christ's command in the biblical tradition by which the church orders its life.

The apostolic commissioning of Matthew 28:19: 'Go, then, to all peoples everywhere and make them my disciples: baptize them in the name of the Father, the Son, and the Holy Spirit' joins with the text of the upper room words of Jesus, given in Luke's and Paul's accounts: 'Do this in memory of me' (Luke 22:19; 1 Cor. 11:24,25) in providing dominical authority for practices of baptizing and celebrating the communion meal. For this reason they are rightly called 'ordinances,' a term which stresses that these acts are ordained by the Lord and appointed to be practised in the church. There may be other laudable ceremonies and time-honoured rituals; but none can be called 'dominical' in precisely the sense that sets apart these two acts. They stand under direct dominical authority – as the church has received it in the canon of scripture; they are free from ancient cultural conditioning and they employ elemental symbols of water, bread and wine. (We may note a contrast with the obviously restricted scope of the command in John 13:15, since 'foot-washing' makes sense *in the precise, detailed way* described in John 13 only in a society which favours open-toed sandals or no foot-covering at all, and knows only unpaved lanes and dusty roads.)[5] Most importantly, both ordinances are the kerygma in action. That is, baptism and the Lord's table bring into focus God's salvation history in a way that could not be said of other 'ordinances,' however valuable they appear to be. Incorporation into Christ – which is the basic meaning of baptism (Gal. 3:27; Rom. 6:1–11; 1 Cor. 12:13) – and a contemporizing of his sacrifice in thanksgiving and renewed participation – which is what the communion service is all about (1 Cor. 10:16, 11:23–32; John 6:52–58): these are the dual 'moments' of grace in which the Lord promises to come to and meet his people.

The word 'ordinance' looks to the church's seeking a mandate to continue these practices. 'Sacrament' is a Latin term for what is 'sacred' or 'set apart.' In its original (dictionary) meaning it referred to a sum of money used as a down-payment. Then it became associated with a soldier's sacred oath of allegiance, and so it came to mean a pledge of religious affiliation. It carries that sense in 1 Peter 3:21: 'a promise made to God' (though the Greek term has other meanings) by the person being baptized. So 'sacrament,' like 'ordinance' or 'means of grace' has a neutral flavour. It simply calls attention to what is hallowed as a church practice and in the sight of God. The Latin version of Ephesians 5:32 gives *sacramentum* of the institution of marriage: 'it is a great truth' or mystery revealed. That is, marriage is a God-honouring, because God-honoured, estate (so Heb. 13:4) and he blesses it with his favour.

Why then is the term 'sacrament' frowned on by some Christians? The answer will come as we sketch the history of how Christ's presence in the ordinances (mainly the Lord's Table service) has been understood.

Signs, Symbols and Sacraments

Both baptism and the Lord's Supper service move in the world of acted or prophetic symbolism that is familiar to us from the practices of the Old Testament. Israel's prophets enforced the spoken word with which they were charged by a dramatization of their message. Sometimes the action was bizarre and unseemly: Ezekiel ate a scroll (Ezek. 3:1–3), lay on his side for more than a year, and cooked his food over excrement (4:4–17). At other times a violent action was a token of divine judgment (Jer. 19:10–15). Occasionally the scene is tender and appealing, as when Hosea reclaimed Gomer from her wilful ways as a sign of Yahweh's patience and forgiving love for his people (Hos. 1:2–11, ch. 3).

a. In baptism the church is faced with the dramatic actions of washing, cleansing and a break with an old life as a prelude to a new beginning. Whether this is directly related to Jewish conversion-baptisms available to proselytes or to John the Baptist's call to penitence, the fact remains that as far as we can trace back Christian initiation has always included, along with the summons to repentance and trust in God's action in Christ, the invitation to accept baptism as a token of incorporation into Christ. Incidental references such as Acts 2:38, 8:12, 36–38, 9:18, 10:48, 16:33, 18:8 are all the more telling for their almost casual narration. Even when no previous instruction has been given, it seems a natural expression of coming to faith to have that experience vividly dramatized in baptism. And Paul has longer theological expositions of the rite in Romans 6:1–11; Galatians 3:26–29 and Colossians 2:11–15.

In the sum, baptism is a focal point in human experience in which God's grace and human response interface; and the dramatic symbolism of water takes on a richer meaning than the merely pictorial and paradigmatic. Baptism is a moment when divine grace is actualized in a human life which is open to its influence and inflow – hence the importance and necessity of faith – and the revelation that came to the Lord in his Jordan baptism (Mark 1:9–11 and parallels) is re-enacted in terms of sonship and Spirit-filling in the experience of his followers. There is of course a unique element in Jesus' baptism that belongs to his unshared filial relationship to the Father; but it is still true that his baptism became a prototype for his church's re-living of the moment of consecration. Since it is his risen life that provides the sphere of our incorporation, it is not incongruous for the New Testament writer to state: '[Baptism] saves you through the resurrection of Jesus Christ' (1 Pet. 3:21). A Christian's baptism is then *not simply a symbol: it conveys the reality it represents within the encompassing experience of grace and faith.*

b. Prophetic dynamism lies equally at the heart of the Lord's Supper. The locus of revelation is seen not only in the bread and the cup, but in the bread *broken* and the wine *poured out*. What Jesus did and what he said go together, since the actions and the interpreting words are complementary and intertwined. The Old Testament background (in Ex.

12 and Deut. 16:1–8 as interpreted and 'targumized' [i.e. explained and brought over into the present] in the Passover *seder* in Judaism) provides us with a vital key to all that the upper room has meant in Christian reflection. It is a sad fact that in the long, tortuous history of eucharistic controversy the Jewish elements in the sacrament have often been lost sight of. The result is an arid debate in philosophical terms about 'accidents,' substance and the 'real presence,' which has largely ignored how Jesus the Jew might have thought of his final meal and impending sacrifice and how he proposed to clarify its meaning to his Jewish disciples gathered around the Passover table.

The dishes in the Passover meal itself are clearly meant as 'signs'; they relate the Jewish participants to the experience of their forebears in the land of Egypt, and vividly portray God's acts in setting his people free. The 'bread of affliction' is a powerful recall of bitter bondage; the several cups dramatize both thanksgiving and expectation just as the Sabbath evening *kiddush* sanctifies the day 'in remembrance of the exodus from Egypt.' But for the Hebrew mind 'symbolism' carries a dynamic nuance. The past is recalled and re-lived. 'Remembering' takes on a sense much richer and more existential than having a past event in mind. There is a way in which past events can be so recreated and charged with potency and effect that their past significance is actualized in the present. For illustration, the harrowing cry of the woman of Zarephath may be mentioned. Her allegation against Elijah was that his visit has been a fateful one: 'Did you come here to remind God of my sins and so cause my son's death?' (1 Kings 17:18). Notice how 'remembering' her past sin is thought of as producing a powerful effect on her life in killing her son.

'This do in remembrance of me' may suggestively be understood in the same dynamic fashion. As the followers of Jesus thereafter will break the bread and pour the wine, what is symbolized in these actions takes on present meaning and is brought out of the historical past (his death on the cross as a sacrifice) and given present efficacy and availability. Paul expresses the same idea: the bread and the cup are the means of sharing in the body and blood of Christ (1 Cor. 10:16).

And the living Christ comes out of a historical frame to meet his people in the present in the sacramental (i.e. the dynamic, realistic) action of what is done in obedience to his express command.

From Motza to Marburg: Eucharistic Presence across the Centuries

'[They] explained to them what had happened on the road, and how they had recognized the Lord when he broke the bread' (Luke 24:35). This is the sequel to the story of the encounter between the Easter Lord and two unknown disciples. It could be regarded simply as the most beautiful story in the gospel sometimes praised as 'the most beautiful book in the world.'[6] But that would be to damn both narrative and gospel with faint praise. Luke's interest is not literary, though he is a considerable *littérateur*. His purpose has at least one ruling motif, which is to clamp together the past life of Jesus and his followers and the generation of Christian believers in his own day. His aim is to make Jesus contemporary with his church.

The Emmaus account serves that purpose at its high point. In the village home of Emmaus – and of all the possible identifications[7] Motza-Colonia some 6.5 kilometres (4 miles) from Jerusalem, which makes feasible the double journey of Luke 24:13,33, seems the most probable – Jesus made his presence real at the meal-table (24:31). All subsequent generations of Christian believers would assent to the reality there described: Christ is made known in the sacrament. The burning issue is: how does he do it? What precisely do Christians need to bring to such a service at which they expect to meet their Lord? What 'power' if any does the consecration of bread and cup have to actualize the divine presence?

In a considerable segment of Christendom the answers are found along lines of 'sacramental efficacy.' Traditional Catholic teaching stresses the power of the act of consecration, so that the bread is set apart by a formula spoken by the priest,[8] and is to be received as the body of the Lord which is what it has become for the faithful. 'Transubstantiation' defines the change that is wrought by the power of the consecrating words, 'This is my body.'

At the Protestant Reformation this teaching was seriously questioned and attacked, but with differing emphases on the meaning of the supper. Luther continued to incline to the traditional Catholic view of the mass, wishing only to reform it, not abolish it. He offered in place of the Roman understanding of Christ's real presence a variant idea that stressed 'consubstantiation.' That is, Christ's objective presence is given 'in, with, and under' the elements of bread and wine. Luther rejected the need for priestly activity to consecrate the body and blood of Christ in the elements, but still he asserted a real participation of the faithful in Christ conveyed through Christ's body which was thought to be everywhere.

Zwingli's views are associated with the notion of a 'spiritualized' reception of the divine presence, since he argued at the Marburg conference, convened by Philip of Hesse in 1529, that the words 'This is my body' are to be understood metaphorically, not literally (as Luther was doing).

Calvin's line was a middle one. 'He rejected Luther's doctrine of "Consubstantiation," and agreed with Zwingli in denying that the Supper was a sacrifice. On the other hand, he sympathized with Luther's desire to insist on the believer's real participation in the Lord's body and blood, and felt Zwingli's comparative lack of emphasis on this aspect so keenly as to describe his doctrine on one occasion as "profane." His own somewhat subtle theory was that the reality of the participation in the body and blood was guaranteed, not by their physical or corporeal presence, but by their dynamic effect on the soul of the participant.'[9]

It is true that modern historical scholarship about Zwingli has accounted for his negative statements on the grounds of his involvement in controversy, and has shown that Zwingli and Calvin differed more in emphasis than in substance. In positive affirmations 'there was nothing to choose between the two great Swiss reformers,' it is alleged.[10]

Nonetheless it still remains that Zwingli was nervous about attaching much more to the sacrament than the function of a commemorative service. Reasons for that reluctance may help to explain his position, but it cannot so easily be contended that this is the Pauline teaching. Nor if we place the upper room meal in a Passover setting can Jesus' mind be explored as though he thought of 'a simple commemorative symbol with the sacred potency belonging to it.'[11] The 'potency' factor lifts the power of the rite out of the realm of memorialism and sets it firmly in the framework of dynamic Hebrew realism. As faithful Jews were encouraged to re-live the Exodus experience and enter into a personal union with their forebears in Egypt by their eating and drinking the paschal dishes and cups, so the children of the new exodus are invited to experience the 'real presence' of the once crucified, now living Lord who comes to them at his table.

'Christ, our Passover lamb, has been sacrified' is a statement that lays the foundation for the apostolic call: 'Our Passover Festival is ready' (1 Cor. 5:7). 'Let us celebrate our Passover,' Paul continues. Provided we do so with 'the bread of purity and truth' – hence Calvin's rightful insistence on a 'worthy reception' – this simple meal can be an occasion of encounter and communion with the risen Lord. His body is there in the bread, not materially or physically (no more than Deut. 16:3 suggests a literal identity with the *matzoth* of Moses' time). Traditional Catholic and Lutheran teaching errs by claiming too much. Yet the reality of his presence is not conveyed in mental reflection. The so-called Zwinglian memorialism is content with too little, since signs and symbols point beyond themselves yet share in the reality they represent, and stimulate and evoke it.[12] Calvin made a concrete insistence on the presence of the body and the blood of Christ, and emphasized – rightly, to be sure – the description of the rite as eating and drinking with a view to communion (see John 6 as well as 1 Cor. 10:16,17). This 'worthy reception' is linked with the activity of the Holy Spirit who uses the bread and wine as carriers or conveyance of the divine presence, made real to the believer in every age. So it may be said that nothing

> Can with this single Truth compare –
> That God was Man in Palestine
> And lives today in Bread and Wine.[13]

7
Will The Church Ever Be One?

A Blueprint for Unity?

Probably the most vexatious question before Christians as they consider the subject of the church and its place in society has to do with relations with other Christians. By common consent they desire, in their best moments of reflection and resolve, a church that comes somewhere near to the ideal of 'one church' in the mind of the Lord. After all, we would readily concede at least in principle, it is *his* church, not ours; it belongs to him and the fact we refer to the church by qualifying adjectives such as Anglican, Methodist, Reformed, Baptist . . . or Roman, Orthodox, Armenian is a matter for regret, however much it has become customary and convenient. 'I will build my church' (Matt. 16:18) is a statement that has an old-fashioned ring about it . . . since who will presume to claim that his branch of the church today is the one Christ is building to the exclusion of other sections (or factions)? Just where is the church to be found? And how may present-day believers, faced with a bewildering array of different 'churches,' ever discover what the Lord's mind for his people might be? The unity of the church is an article of credal confession ('one holy catholic apostolic church'); how can it become a down-to-earth reality? Will the 'scandal' of 'our unhappy divisions' ever be resolved?

John's gospel contains a passage (ch. 17) that is surely relevant to this problem. Here, if anywhere in the New Testament, we are offered the mind of the Lord for his people. This prayer has rightly been called 'Jesus' last will'[1] for his church; it is couched in the prayer-speech of intercession. Using language reminiscent of the vocabulary employed throughout the Fourth Gospel – with key terms such as 'glory,' 'eternal life,' 'world,' 'truth' – and frankly confessional (verse 3, which contains the speaker's own name in full), Jesus utters a threefold supplication on his triumphant road to the cross and his exaltation. He prays for himself (verses 1–8); he has his immediate disciples in view (verses 9–19); and his embrace reaches out to Christians in subsequent ages (verses 20–26).[2]

It is the last section that has caught current imagination and fired enthusiasm for Christian unity. 'I pray that they may all be one' (verse 21) is a banner under which several movements towards organic unity have been launched, perhaps with little regard for the need to set this single text within the context of its passage and to interpret it on a canvas that features other important ideas as well.

In 1689 *The True Nature of a Gospel Church* by John Owen, the Puritan divine and church leader, appeared posthumously. John 17 is best described by that title. There are five parts to it.

The Testament of Jesus

a. The church of John 17 is a community with definable perimeters. Jesus speaks of 'those you gave me out of the world. They belonged to you and you gave them to me' (verse 6). The idiom in this description of the disciples may be Johannine ('out of the word,' 'you gave them'),[3] but the basic idea is surely common to the gospels as a whole, as we have observed. There is an acknowledgement of the Father's claim on his creation; God is Lord of human lives which is a fundamental postulate of Jesus' recorded teaching about the kingdom of God. There is a celebration of his gift (cf. Luke 12:32), whether of the kingdom or of those who enter that kingdom in response to Jesus' call, 'Follow me'. The fact of revelation is recognised, as the prayer continues in verse 8: 'I gave them the message that you gave me and they received it' – a thought that is parallel to the great 'cry of joy' in Matthew 11:25–27 = Luke 10:21,22, and gives us insight into Jesus' mission as the one who bodies forth the divine presence and reveals the heart of God the Father, the *Abba* of family intimacy.

This description also implies several other important notions about the church. It fixes the contours as centred on Christ and defines limits of those who belong to the church as those who belong to him. This picture would give justification for the label 'the gathered church,' since like Israel of the old covenant, this is a 'purchased people,' called 'my people' by Yahweh and redeemed from alien dominion (Ex. 3:7,10, 15:13,16) to be Yahweh's personal property, his *segullah*, a word with overtones of exclusive possession (Ex. 19:5,6).[4] The obvious distinction is that now it is messiah's people, 'my church,' claimed as his since these disciples are the Father's gift to his Son (John 6:37). Yet this affirmation has a shadow side (John 6:65,70).

As with old Israel, the heart of this mystery is election – another Johannine motif, but it is common New Testament teaching that surfaces in the Old Testament language of passages like Romans 9:23–26; 1 Peter 1:2, 2:4–10 and Revelation 1:4–6. The elect people of God are called into being as a historical witness to the Father's pleasure with his Son Jesus Christ who is the elect one par excellence. They are his church because he is God's messiah, and messiah must have a people, 'the kingdom of the saints of the most High' (Dan. 7). Their calling is to membership in his body; their vocation is to serve him. This is the focal point of the church's unity, concealed from public view yet a reality in God's age-old plan to honour his beloved Son with a people for his own possession.

b. The lesson from the martyrs in Daniel's time was one the disciples of Jesus were slow to appreciate. The exaltation of the Son of man to be head of a world empire (Dan. 7:13–27) was welcome news, especially if it included them as partners and sharers in Jesus' enterprise of kingdom-building. Hence the incident of Mark 10:35–45 is typically in character. James and John are simply drawing logical conclusions from the announcement, 'We are going up to Jerusalem' (Mark 10:33), conveniently stopping their ears against Jesus' following predictions of a passion and a bloody fate. They think of baptism only as a prelude to the coming of a glorious kingdom, and a cup drunk in festivity and triumph. They, like the rest, need the solemn assurance that Jesus' victory is achieved in suffering; there is no crown without a cross.

Jesus' disciples in subsequent ages need the same reminder, for the lesson is hard to learn. Twice repeated, though with a stylistic variation, comes the pledge from the church's servant-messiah: 'keep them safe . . . I kept them safe (the Greek verb is *tēreō*, to treasure, to keep close as a cherished possession as in John 12:7) . . . I protected them' (the Greek is *phylassō*, to keep intact or safe, as a prisoner is kept in gaol). These statements are in John 17 verses 11,12; and verse 15 turns the thought into a second, more pointed prayer, 'I do ask you to keep them safe from the Evil One.'

The danger is clear. The seduction of the evil one is ever to avoid the cross; in the mouth of Simon Peter, it is heard crying, 'God forbid it, Lord! This must never happen to you!' (Matt. 16:22), when the destiny of both messiah and messiah's people looms into view. Now Jesus senses the snare. He himself has unmasked the satan that prompted Peter's rebuke. In turn he rebuked Peter. Now the Johannine Christ prays that his people in times to come may realize how this particular temptation will need to be faced and conquered in the long haul of church history. From delusions of earthly grandeur, from striving for terrestrial power and worldly clout, from all easy roads to success that bypass the cross as a daily commitment (Luke 9:23) and an accepted way of life (2 Cor. 4:10–12, 12:10) this petition calls for deliverance. And the same prayer gives reason for security, since it recalls us to the secret of the church's sustenance and true growth as it follows the way of the cross to triumph beyond suffering and defeat.

c. The distinguishing marks of the church in Jesus' great prayer have already been elaborated in the Fourth Gospel. While it is true that the word church is not found in this gospel, and there is no counterpart (except at 6:67–69) to the incident at Caesarea Philippi, it would be wrong to conclude that the gospel of John lacks the idea of the church and that John is preoccupied only with personal relationships with

Jesus to the exclusion of a corporate union.[5] Explicit references to Jesus' purpose 'to bring together into one body all
the scattered children of God' (11:52) and to draw all men
to himself (12:32) suggest exactly the church idea, as does the
consistent Johannine theme of the new temple which is the
Lord's body, refashioned on the third day of his being raised
(2:18–22).

The sub-surface teaching is just as impressive. Jesus is the
centre of his flock which is closely knit around him
(10:11–16, 27–30) and as they follow him, his design is to
create 'one flock' under one shepherd. The theological comment in 10:29,30 recalls that both the shepherd's care and the
sheep which are protected are realities grounded deep within
the eternal counsels of God. The statement, 'The Father and
I are one' (verse 30) is the theological undergirding for the
unity of the church as messiah's flock.

The same conclusion stands in John 15. As the imagery
changes, though still Palestinian agrarian in setting, we hear
of one vine. Again kinship with old Israel is obvious to the
reader of Psalm 80:8–19; Isaiah 5:1–7; Jeremiah 2:21; and
Hosea 10:1 (cf. 4 Ezra 5:23). There are many separate
branches (verse 3), yet a common life runs through trunk
and branches, and 'union' with the source of that life is the
secret of fruitfulness and a productive crop. The emphasis
falls on 'remaining' since it is only by maintaining a living
contact that growth is possible. Organic life flows through
the vine and out to the branches so that the greatest disaster
is to be severed from the root.

This teaching is made clear in Jesus' prayer. He asks that
his life may unite all his people as they share his redemptive
purpose (17:11). He prays that 'they may all be one' with a
unity that is modelled on the mutual interpenetration of the
divine life uniting Father and Son (verse 21). The Father sent
the Son; the Son is always obedient in filial joy (John 5:19,
8:29). There is a mutuality that reaches back to eternity
(1:1–18) and finds expression within the time-frame in terms
of what the Father willed and how Jesus gladly accepted that
will.

John 6:36–40 succinctly expresses this coinherence
between God and Jesus. It is summed up in typically Johan-

nine fashion with an I-word: 'I have come down from heaven to do the will of him who sent me, not my own will.' The Father's will is the salvation of the world (3:16,17). The Son is the willing – and indispensable because the unique – accomplice. They are 'one' (5:26, 10:30), and in a daring re-wording of the Gethsemane story Jesus declares an almost effortless obedience to the end (18:11 : 'Do you think that I will not drink the cup of suffering my Father has given me?'). He then moves onwards in his triumphal march to the cross and his glory-in-suffering. This is the unity of John 17:21, so much to be desired that it becomes a paradigm of how the church should be 'one.'

How can this be? Taking a cue from the earlier insistence that there is complete unanimity in the divine enterprise to save the world, we may see John's understanding of *unity as expressed in a common purpose and a shared goal*. The focal point of unity is the mission that brought Jesus from the Father's presence and led him back there, carrying as the fruits of his passion those whom God had given him (17:22–26). The 'ontological' union between God and the Word (in the prologue of 1:1–18) is the deep foundation; the missiological consequence flows from it, for it is the Father's active will to reclaim the world by sending his Son. The ecclesiological dimension is seen in how Christians respond to the challenge of the unfinished agenda ('As the Father sent me, so I send you,' 20:21) of a world that still needs to see the love of God in Christ and in Christ's people and be drawn to it.

d. 'Mission' is thus the order of the day in the church's continuing calendar. The Johannine charter matches this vocation exactly: 'I sent them into the world just as you sent me into the world' (17:18). John has already made clear the interconnection that binds together God, Jesus and the disciples. In a saying that recalls the earlier gospels, Jesus remarks: 'I tell you the truth: whoever receives anyone I send, receives me also; and whoever receives me, receives him who sent me' (13:20; Matt. 10:40,41; Luke 9:48; negatively Luke 10:16).

We notice how the oneness of his people is intimately tied

to the effectiveness of their continuing mission. This suggests a double parallel. Father and Son are in complete accord and this unanimity is expressed historically, concretely in the Father's sending and the Son's being sent. So it is to be with the church. 'That the world may know' (verse 23) and so 'will believe that you sent me' (verse 21), the church is called to its unity. The inference is that *its* mission too will be credible in the eyes of the world only as it represents and conveys unity-in-truth and makes concrete the heavenly reality of its union with the Father and the Son. John is wrestling here with a problem that has haunted the pages of church history ever since his day. How can the life of the church adequately validate the claim of the church to be a society whose life is in God? When there are so many disfiguring blemishes and stains to mar the image, how can the mission of God in the church and through the church to the world ever be believable?

The letters of John are a sad record of unlovely professing Christians (1 John 3:15,17), power-hungry ecclesiastics like Diotrephes (3 John 9,10) and deceivers who deny the Lord in the name of a 'progressivism' that does not abide in the teaching of Christ (2 John 7–11). Surely this dismal picture immediately discounts any pretension to fulfil the calling ascribed in John 17. But happily this is not the complete story.

In the same letters we meet Demetrius who is well commended even by the Lord himself (3 John 12) as well as by the Elder. Gaius has a similar character reference (3 John 1–4). Also we hear the apostolic witness behind these documents that summons their readers to teaching with an unmistakable ring: 'Let us love one another . . . whoever lives in love lives in God and God lives in him . . . You must all live in love' (1 John 4:7,16; 2 John 6). And, not surprisingly, out of this treasured relationship of love to God and one's fellow believer come the true missionary spirit and example (3 John 5–7).

e. The Johannine community is called to live in a hostile world.[6] 'The world hated them' (17:14). This antagonistic note pervades the gospel, since Jesus is constantly threatened, especially in Jerusalem, by alien powers that seek to destroy him. 'Why are you trying to kill me?' he asks at the Feast of Tabernacles as he teaches in the Temple Court (7:19). At a later festival, again in the holy city, the threat is shown to be no idle one. 'Then the Jews once more picked up stones to throw at him' (10:31), judging his teaching to be that of a blasphemer who deserved to be punished in the prescribed manner. Thomas the Twin senses the danger of yet another visit to Jerusalem, that it will seal their fate: 'Let us all go along with the Teacher, that we may die together with him!' (11:16).

Sadly, the same destiny is in store for the church that follows closely the road marked out by its faithful Lord. 'If they persecuted me, they will persecute you too' (15:20). The hypothetical form of the statement is only too ominous. The world has shown its hatred to both Father and Son (15:24), and there can be no question that the church will receive its share of suffering and abuse in a world which although still loved by God yet is opposed to his sovereign will. In John's teaching there is a deep cleavage, amounting almost to a dualism, between God and the world (1 John 5:19 : 'the whole world is under the rule of the Evil One'). So opposition and hatred are to be expected, and there is no avoiding the conflict.

But to anticipate and face the struggle is only part of the prospect. There is also reassurance and hope: 'This is how we win the victory over the world: with our faith. Who can defeat the world? Only he who believes that Jesus is the Son of God' (1 John 5:4,5; Rev. 2:7,11,17, 3:12,21, 12:10,11, 17:14). For John even worse than to succumb in the conflict is to go over to the other side. Hence the stringent warnings of 1 John 2:15–17, concluding with the real reason for the Christian hope. That hope is· cast upon eternal life, begun now and destined to last, whereas 'the world is passing away.' So by a strong faith in Christ's victory (John 16:33: 'I have defeated the world!') and with a confidence set in the eternal world to which the glorious Lord leads his own (John 17:24–26), the militant church faces all the venom and hostility of a cruel and cynical world, peopled by types such as Caiaphas (11:49,50, 18:14) and the emperors Nero and Domitian (Rev. 13:18, 17:9–14, 19:16); and it comes through victorious, if not in this world then in the world where Christ's glory is displayed (17:24; Rev. 3:21).

Some Lessons: Then and Now

It remains now to draw out some conclusions from this study as we attempt to apply, as far as possible, this presentation of the church in John 17 to our scene today. The main features of the Johannine church are clearly visible, though we may hesitate to follow E. Käsemann in his description of that community as a conventicle removed from the world and opposed to all churchly structures.[7]

The 'photo-kit' picture offered in these few verses has sharply drawn lines separating the church from 'the world'. In John's day the world was the great enemy since the term stood for anti-God forces that threatened to overwhelm the community in Asia Minor. On the one hand there was the danger of a gnostic take-over, equated with the error of docetism which denied the true humanity of the earthly Jesus. On the other was the imperial power which exerted pressure on Christians to compromise their loyalty to Jesus Christ as sole Lord.[8] The emperor Domitian (AD 81–96) was proclaimed as 'our lord and god,' and honoured in temples erected in Ephesus and Pergamum in Roman Asia, and this arrogant claim would certainly pose a threat to the Johannine communities in the nearby province. On both counts there was need to mark out clearly the claims of faith and unbelief whether pseudo-Christian or anti-God.

Much of this presentation of church life is shaped by these factors, as the Johannine church recalls its Lord's mind to fashion a society having a clear self-awareness as his people. It lives out its life and exerts its influence in a way that shows how it treads the way of the cross in suffering (as in the book called the Revelation). It finds its centre of unity in truth and in love for God and the brethren. Its mission is to make its proclaimed message credible by its life-style and patient endurance under trial. These are the 'notes' that distinguish the church of John's day.

With a little imagination and some transposition it is not

difficult to see the present-day relevance of this 'identi-kit' specimen. Anti-Christian political structures still threaten to entice the church from its sole allegiance to Jesus Christ and to mute its witness to the only rightful 'King of kings and Lord of lords' (Rev. 19:16). There is still great need for courage and stability in the face of threats and real suffering. And so Jesus' prayers for his people are timely.

More problematic is the question of how the faith is to be confessed and the church's message shaped to meet the needs of our day. There were those in John's church who found no difficulty in a truncated message attempting to accommodate the person of Christ to a gnostic system; and they are branded as 'going beyond' the teaching of the Lord (2 John 9). At a different level, but possibly associated with such 'false prophets' (1 John 4:1–6), is the case of Diotrephes in 3 John. He 'loves to be [a] leader' and to set himself up in a prominent place from which he defames the apostolic authority of the Johannine circle (3 John 10). He has definite ideas about who should be in the church and who ought to be expelled. He is a clear exponent of a 'pure church' theory!

John has no alternative but to denounce him, and he minces no words about the avoidance of 'the spirit of error' (1 John 4:6). But what he writes in his proverb, 'Do not imitate what is bad, but imitate what is good' (3 John 11) is practised in his own leadership. The anti-christ faction is allowed to leave of its own accord (1 John 2:19); there is no hint of excommunication, even if the lines of demarcation between the church and the world are clearly set, and teachers of error require to be unmasked as 'liars' and 'deceivers.'

Unity-in-truth is the litmus test, where 'truth' is essentially christological and soteriological.[9] Who Jesus Christ was and is directly affects our understanding of his saving work of revelation and redemption. This would be the irreducible minimum of agreed truth: is he confessed and believed as 'true God, true man' and is he the sole saviour of the world and its exalted Lord? Where this is a common platform,[10] mission becomes a co-operative endeavour and indeed is a viable venture. Otherwise Christianity is demoted to one among several competing religions, and there is no dynamic or driving force in the church's effort.

But we should not fail to see the corollary. A robust christology and an uncompromising doctrine of salvation through Christ crucified and victorious will invite opposition and resistance. In the Roman world with its pluralistic tolerance Christianity stood out as offensive, since it proclaimed 'another emperor, Jesus.' In our day a church committed to Jesus' uniqueness and unrivalled claims can expect no less to have its share of suffering. In Jürgen Moltmann's telling phrase, there is 'the apostolate in suffering,' and the church fulfils its role as missionary agent in the world by accepting a destiny of 'participation in the apostolic mission of Christ' that 'leads inescapably into *tribulation, contradiction and suffering.*'[11]

8
The Church and the World

Defining the World

The church of John 17 was, as we have observed, clearly distinguished from the surrounding 'world.' The last term is ambivalent, even within the pages of the Johannine writings. (i) Sometimes 'world' stands for the human race to which God sent the Son as his gracious gift: 'The Father sent his Son to be the Saviour of the world' (1 John 4:14). Moreover this mission was an expression of his heart of love (John 3:16) and that coming from God into the world was an errand of mercy, not judgment (John 3:17).

The same term shades off (ii) into the idea of the sphere of God's creation. God made the world through the pre-existing logos, and he came at his birth to be 'in the world' (John 1:10) where he shone as its light (John 8:12, 9:5: 'While I am in the world I am the light for the world'). The transition is made here from 'the world as created' to (iii) the thought of the moral universe peopled by men and women who are in the darkness. A favourite Johannine theme is this stark contrast, though it is paralleled among sectarian Jewish groups in first-century Judaism. The children of light are there opposed by the children of darkness.

The adherents of John's church rejoiced in their being 'in the light' (1 John 1:7, 2:8) and so marked off from the 'world' which was their great enemy. The astringent counsel is therefore to be expected: 'Do not love the world' (1 John 2:15) for reasons that are then supplied. This 'world' is society antagonistic to God, bounded by temporal limits and characterized by sensual practices which are to be shunned at all costs.

Three characteristics are given by John. The 'world' (in this third connotation) is (*a*) what the sinful self – the 'flesh' of Romans 7 and Galatians 5:19 to give it a broader scope – desires; (*b*) what people see and want – the lure of material possessions that so easily provokes an insatiable craving to have things within our grasp; and (*c*) everything in this world that people are proud of. These items together constitute the world which is 'not of the Father' and is doomed to disappear with the passage of time. So 1 John 2:15–17 make clear. This is the 'world' usually referred to in the antithesis of the 'church and the world,' though we mistake what appear to be clear-cut lines of division if we suppose that there were no problem cases for the first Christians. One example is 1 Corinthians 5:9,10 where Paul's earlier ruling not to associate with immoral people (a warning preserved maybe in 2 Cor. 6:14–7:1) had been misunderstood and misapplied as though it referred to the world of the Corinthians' *pagan* neighbours. 'To avoid them you would have to get out of the world completely!' (verse 10*b*) – leading to an abandonment of the world Paul never seems to have envisaged, even if it is true that 'this world, as it is now, will not last much longer' (1 Cor. 7:31).

But in the main there were clear lines of distinction to separate the early Christians from their non-Christian contemporaries, as we shall see.

The Church's Self-Awareness

The church that meets us in the pages of the New Testament had a clear self-conscious identity, standing over against the pagan world. An almost casual aside from Paul throws light on this. 'Live in such a way as to cause no trouble either to Jews or Greeks, or to the church of God' – neither Jewish nor Gentile but Christian. Already the seeds of the later idea of the church as a 'third race' are there in the New Testament (1 Cor. 10:32).

a. Paul, Peter, the writer of Hebrews and John – the chief witnesses in the New Testament apostolic literature – all concur with the affirmation that at conversion believers enter upon a new life and set their faces in a fresh direction. 'When anyone is joined to Christ he is a new being: the old is gone, the new has come. All this is done by God' (2 Cor. 5:17,18) could be the theme-song of these exponents of the Christian life in their diverse communities. The language and its idioms may differ; but the reality of 'once you were that . . . now you are this' remains. Some samples may be given.

The Galatians had known a mighty transformation wrought by God and accompanied by the gifts of the Spirit (Gal. 3:3,4). They had been liberated from the pull of 'this present evil age' (1:4) and placed in the sphere of Christ's lordship (5:24) as members of God's family (4:6,7) and sharers in a new order of society, quite unheard-of in the world around them (3:26–29). Even sex inequalities, racial barriers and social stratifications were to yield before the prospect of membership of this new order – 'all one in Christ Jesus' (so too Col. 3:10–12,15; Eph. 2:11–22). The letter to Philemon gives a concrete illustration, especially verse 16.

Images such as transference to a new kingdom (Col. 1:13,14); emergence out of darkness into light (Eph. 5:8,14); deliverance from wrath to reconciliation with God (1 Thess. 4:9; Rom. 5:6–11) and freedom from superstition and fear to a new-found confidence in God (Gal. 4:8,9; Rom. 8:15–17) – these are only some of the ways the change is described.[1]

Paul ransacks language to express the new life that flows from an initial union with Christ and baptism into his body the church. On one side is the dark 'world' – under the tyranny of evil and bad religion, dark with fears and forebodings, subject to divine judgment (Rom. 1:18–32) and holding men and women in the grip of superstition, vicious habits and base ways (Gal. 4:10; Col. 2:21; 1 Cor. 6:9–11). On the other side of the divide is all that is implied in 'being-in-Christ' and one with his people. True, many of Paul's converts were slow learners; others were wilful children, quickly deserting his gospel at the least provocation; still others perverted his teaching and misheard his message of 'free grace' by supposing it to be an invitation to licence and libertinism (Rom. 3:8, 6:1). But there were those who grasped the implications of his preaching and embarked on a new way of life. Surely more Christians than only the

Philippians and the Thessalonians turned out to be 'his joy and crown' (Phil. 4:1; 1 Thess. 2:19), even if only they are explicitly praised in this way.

Peter, in shorter compass, makes the same contrast between the 'former ways' of his converts (1 Pet. 1:14) and the new life-style marked out by holiness (1:15) and dedication to the Lord (3:15) to be the new Israel of God (2:1–10). Nor is the motif 'no longer this' absent from Peter (4: 2,3), as he summons his readers to have done with past habits and to live according to 'the true grace of God.' 'Stand firm in it' is his rousing climax (5:12) to a hortatory appeal, directed (it may be) to recently baptized Christians as they set out on a new road as 'newborn' people (2:2).[2]

The addressees of *Hebrews* were evidently Christians much further along the road of Christian pilgrimage. Their great danger was that of weariness and disappointment at the hardness of the path and the lengthy interval before they should reach the heavenly city (10:35–39). This explains the warnings and appeals that punctuate the letter which again (as 1 Peter) reads more like a sermon than a treatise or formal epistle. The writer's literary style agrees with his method of approach. He will remind the hearers of what they were before becoming Christians and citizens of the new commonwealth. He does so by recalling the marvellous gifts of their 'enlightenment' (6:4). Then they 'tasted heaven's gift and received their share of the Holy Spirit. They knew from experience that God's word is good and they felt the powers of the coming age' (6:4,5). How can they abandon all this, and fall away? They must not be 'people who turn back and are lost' (10:39). Apostasy was a very real peril, fraught with fearful consequences (10:26–31).[3] But our author is confident that his appeal will not remain unheeded (6:9); rather they will go on to obtain their great reward (10:35). Obviously they had crossed over the line separating their 'old life,' and were responding to their pilgrim vocation as God's people on the march. The thrust of the writer's call is, 'Don't go back.' Rather, 'Let us go forward' (6:1).

John, as we saw, makes probably the strongest insistence on the demarcation line between the church and the world, and reflects a type of church life which is self-contained and possesses clear identity marks which are not found among those 'in the world.' Love for God and love of the fellow-Christian, abiding in Christ and walking in the light, obedience to the commandments and having eternal life – these are all summed up in the claim: 'We know that we belong to God and that the whole world is under the rule of the Evil One' (1 John 5:19).

b. With conversion as an entrée to new life in the Spirit it is not surprising that a person in those far off days was thought of as either *inside* or *outside* the church. Although the former term is not found in so many words, the term 'outside' is: see Mark 4:11; 1 Corinthians 5:12; Colossians 4:5 which all use the same expression (*hoi exō* : those on the outside; 1 Tim. 3:7 has *hoi exōthen* with the same meaning). No half-way position seemed possible.

The lines of distinction were firmly drawn to erect boundaries, though naturally the church was open-ended at the point where its gates were ready to receive enquirers, postulants and those professing to join the company. 'Unbelievers' and 'ordinary persons' (RSV 'outsiders,' Greek *idiōtai*) were evidently permitted to be within earshot of the church assembled for worship (1 Cor. 14:23,24), and they could benefit from the exercise of the gift of prophecy (= pastoral proclamation-in-the-Spirit). There was no 'closed shop,' as though the church were sealed off from the world to form an esoteric enclave like the monks at Qumran in the Judaean desert or the secret societies of the Greek and Roman mystery religions.

The traffic, however, was two-way. If sincere seekers were welcomed – and even those with dubious motives such as Simon in Acts 8:9–24 found a temporary place in the fellowship – it was apparently a procedural discipline to deal drastically with blatant offenders who grievously sinned and dishonoured the purity of the church. For Paul the issues were chiefly in the realm of moral failures, as in the case of the incestuous person at Corinth (1 Cor. 5:1–5).[4] The case was exacerbated by the pride of the Corinthians who rejoiced evidently that only one such case was reported in their midst: hence the Pauline metaphor of 'a little leaven' which makes the whole batch of dough to rise (1 Cor. 5:6). His directive is clear and trenchant. At a congregational meeting, 'You are to hand this man over to Satan for his body (lit. 'his flesh,' the evil impulse that had goaded him into sin; or else a physical chastening is intended as in 2 Cor. 12:7, which Lampe refers to) to be destroyed.' This is an excommunication order, expelling him from the church to the world where Satan holds sway. But the effect is remedial: 'so that his spirit will be saved in the Day of the Lord' (verse 5). The lamentable failure at Corinth was that they had a blind spot; they were concerned to keep themselves detached from the world to the extent of becoming ascetic and world-denying (1 Cor. 5:9,10), yet they were overlooking gross sin in their midst and had failed to apply disciplinary controls. In a measured statement of far-reaching consequence, Paul lays down the dictum: 'it is none of my business to judge outsiders. God will judge them. But should you not judge the members of your own fellowship?' As often, the 'sentence of holy law' is buttressed by a scriptural text: 'Take the evil man out of your group' (verse 13, a reference to Deut. 17:7 which requires the united agreement of two or three witnesses before a fateful sentence is carried out).

Moral lapses are at the root of the severe condemnation meted out to Hymenaeus and Alexander (1 Tim. 1:19,20). They too had insensate consciences and had evidently undercut the strict moral requirements of the Christian life. 'Handing over to Satan' is a similar method of excommunication; and it is applied for ethical aberrations, not doctrinal heterodoxy (though another Hymenaeus is clearly a false teacher in 2 Tim. 2: 17,18).

Deliberate falsification of the word of God does appear in such passages as 2 Corinthians 2:17, 4:2. Paul contrasts his own motives and ministry with 'many others, who handle God's message as if it were cheap merchandise,' either by hawking it around because of a mercenary desire to 'get rich quick' (like the Greek sophists) or watering it down like innkeepers who adulterated wine to make it more plentiful.[5] More seriously still, the intruding teachers, whose message is one of a 'different Jesus' (2 Cor. 11:4) or whose coming to Galatia brought with it 'a gospel that is different from the one we preached' (Gal. 1:8), incur Paul's severest indictments. These men who are no less than 'false apostles' are the devil's servants (2 Cor. 11:15), and their doom is sealed (Gal. 1:9: 'may he be condemned to hell!').

What stands out is the type of preaching that occasioned Paul's outbursts of fierce indignation and condemnation. The two defective elements concern the person of the Lord (which was being demoted at Corinth, possibly in the interest of a docetic christology) and the way of salvation (which was the point at issue with the Galatian Judaizers who insisted on Jewish rituals). Where these cardinal truths were at stake, Paul could be and indeed was unyielding. At the place from which he wrote the Philippian letter the rival preaching was of a lesser concern. It is a matter for some discussion to identify these preachers but Paul's language is more restrained and temperate (Phil. 1:14–18), and he generously concedes that so long as it is Christ who is being proclaimed – even if from unworthy motives – he will rejoice.

The situation reflected in the Pastoral epistles is somewhere midway. True, the verb that is coined – *heterodidaskaleō* (1 Tim. 1:3, 6:3) – suggests at first sight a deviant doctrine, teaching false ideas. But it seems that such preaching was not necessarily contrary to the Pauline gospel. 'It was not so much a question of doctrinal deviations as of the introduction of profane matters (1 Tim. 6:20; 2 Tim. 2:16; cf. Tit. 3:9; 2 Tim. 3:16,17)',[6] and it is the preacher's character – as in Titus 1:10,16; 1 Timothy 4:2; 2 Timothy 3:13 – that is under fire rather than the substance of what is proclaimed.

The 'prophets' in 1 John who advocate a docetic (i.e. humanity-denying) interpretation of the Lord's person are exposed by the Elder and the error of their ways is brought to light. No ban of excommunication follows, however; and it is simply a question of allowing them to leave the Johannine church of their own accord (1 John 2:18–25). The test is self-applied. If they stay, it is a sign of their acceptance of apostolic truth; if they choose to leave, their desire to move beyond the apostolic credo is evident – and this latter course they had elected to take. Interestingly, this mild type of excommunication contrasts with the fierce denunciations of the later 'heretics' whose teaching and practices are reprobated in Jude and 2 Peter, as well as Revelation chapters 2,3. There we may trace a full-blown gnostic libertinism rising to the surface and undermining both the person of Christ and his saving work (2 Pet. 2:1) and the high-toned ethical way of life required of Christians (notice the examples drawn from Sodom and Gomorrah in Jude 7, and the violent language of invective in 2 Pet. 2:21,22). But Paul can resort to bitter irony when his gospel and its moral claims are under fire (Gal. 5: 12: 'Let them [the circumcizers] go on and castrate themselves!'; Phil. 3:2: 'Watch out for . . . those dogs, men who insist on cutting the body').

Possibly the fiercest verdict of judgment levelled at Christians, whether real or pseudo, comes in the story of Ananias and Sapphira (Acts 5:1–11). Their root sin was hypocrisy and a refusal to own up once the deed of their false statement was uncovered, as we have observed (p. 33). Attempts have been made to 'explain' the severity of the judgment and to attribute it mostly to Ananias' impenitence as well as the parallelism of this 'flaw' of the new creation with Adam's primal disobedience in Genesis. Whatever the meaning of the fearful account may be, one thing stands out. The church like old Israel is meant to be a holy society in which the disciplining of failing and hardhearted members follows inexorably. The 'numinous' quality that attended the Jerusalem church (Acts 5:13) fits in precisely with Luke's theme.

Conclusion

The foregoing study adds up to a set of conclusions, deducible from the data. In the New Testament churches membership was seriously regarded, since it is likened to passing 'from death to life' (1 John 3:14). Allegiance both to the Lord or the church and the fellowship of his people was taken to be a lifelong and a life-changing commitment. Lapses, therefore, on the grounds of embracing 'strange' theological notions (especially christological) but more particularly on the score of falling into immoral ways, were stringently and aseptically dealt with – but where penitence and hope of amendment were aroused, as in 2 Corinthians 2:5–11, there was a therapeutic value in the 'short, sharp shock' of a summary discipline. Above all, we find ourselves looking at a set of churches with visible and recognized boundaries, making them distinct from the 'world' around them.

The Church's Response to the World

The picture sketched in our preceding pages represents in the main first- or second-generation Christianity; and it has in view a church that is set in a missionary situation. Paul's preaching was what is termed initial evangelism addressed to those who stood on the fringe of the synagogue as godfearers (according to the specimen example of Acts 13:14–41) or, more obviously once his mission to the Graeco-Roman lands got under way, to men and women who had known only the worship of current pagan divinities. One clear illustration of Paul's message is: 'You turned away from idols to God, to serve the true and living God and to wait for his Son to come from heaven – his Son Jesus, whom he raised from the dead, and who rescues us from God's wrath that is to come' (1 Thess. 1:9,10).[7]

The subsequent letters to the infant church at Thessalonica are full of signs of what this new life was meant to be, including such elementary instructions as how to please God (4:1), how to avoid immorality (4:3–8) and practise monogamy in a pure marriage relationship, and how to love one's fellow Christian (4:9). All this comes from 1 Thessalonians.

With the increasing growth and development of the church in various centres, ethical concerns needed a fuller and more specific spelling out. This led to the rise of the so-called station-codes, first seen in Colossians 3:18–4:1 (the earliest example of how household members – wives, husbands, fathers, children, parents, slaves, masters – were to live together according to their God-appointed 'station' in life). Further elaborations appear in Ephesians 5:22–6:9; 1 Peter 2:18–3:7; Titus 2:1–10; 1 Timothy 2:9–15; and in the later church fathers.

The key idea is submission, though there is a counterbalancing emphasis on reciprocal obligations which is not found in moral maxims, mainly Stoic, outside the New Testament.

Other primary motivations of these calls to obedience and subordination are the glad acceptance of the lordship of Christ – obviously a unique Christian motif; a conscious desire on the part of Christians to pattern their family life on the model of the holy family in Nazareth as recorded in Luke chapters 1, 2 and to 'imitate' the example of the Lord in his humility; and (most convincingly) a restraining influence placed on free-wheeling Christians who imagined that because they were 'saved' they were free from all moral inhibitions. The onset of 'antinomianism' – an ugly name for an equally obnoxious practice, implying an abandoning of all moral restrictions on the score that Christians were 'free from the law' and so at liberty to please themselves – came early in church history; and its presence led to the formulating of ethical behaviour patterns designed to regulate how Christians should live 'in this world' in a way consonant with their profession.

Unhappily a well-intentioned desire to set out guidelines led to legalism. Christians began to think of their faith in Christ as a 'new law,' and by a back-door the very impositions that Paul had strenuously rebutted in Galatia and at Philippi and Corinth were readmitted. The gospel of Matthew shows how easily the good news could be misunderstood – if it is the case that its rigorism, its call to perfection, its exalting of the 'law of Christ' and its discipline were calculated to offset a mistaken overemphasis on free grace by some of Paul's enthusiastic followers after his death. Matthew's needful stress in those places where it records Jesus' teaching in 3:15, 5:17–20, 5:48, 7:20,24–27, 11:28–30, 28:20 could so easily be taken to the opposite extreme; and this indeed happened as Christians, preferring Matthew to the other gospels, tended to treat it as a law-book containing a set of codified ethics. The next step was a fateful one. The church took on organizational form, with all the hallmarks of a regulated society. The age of the institutional church had arrived. The church became habituated in the world, and settled down to order its life in society often by adopting the behaviour patterns of that society.

Church and State

The next important step was, however, the result of political and social pressures. After a time of intense struggle with the authorities of the Roman empire and the enduring of several traumatic state persecutions, a new day dawned with the 'conversion' of the emperor Constantine in AD 312. To understand the significance of this event, we have to recall how in the intervening centuries between the end of the first century and the commencement of the fourth, the organized church had grown in numerical strength and social acceptance. And there was always the possibility of hostility between church and state breaking out. We need, however, to begin with the *New Testament teaching on the state.*

In Romans 13:1–7 Paul had expressed thankfulness for the good order that prevailed in the early part of the emperor Nero's principate, thanks to Roman law and social justice. 'The existing authorities have been put there by God . . . the ruler [magistrate] is God's servant working for your own good. . . . He is God's servant and carries out God's wrath on the one who does evil. For this reason you must obey the authorities . . . and pay taxes, for the authorities are working for God when they fulfil their duties.' These sentiments have a specific historical background in view, and do not formulate a philosophy of 'good government' that is applicable for all time and in every circumstance. Paul and Peter (in 1 Pet. 2:13–17) were only too thankful to have Roman law and order on their side in the years prior to Nero's change of front. The situation in AD 64–65 altered all that; and with Nero's pogrom launched against Christians in Rome following the great fire and the subsequent martyr deaths of the leading apostles, the character of the state changed from benign neutrality or passive indifference to active opposition.

There were several factors that led to this altered situation. Not least was a clearly expressed claim to divinity on the part of some Roman emperors in their lifetime (especially Domitian, AD 81–96) and a mounting fear that the physical growth and social importance of the church posed a threat to the security of the state – a trend seen in Trajan's time (AD 98–117) and visible in his correspondence with the

Bithynian governor Pliny. Thereafter a succession of 'persecuting emperors' followed; and the church's hardening attitude of resistance as well as an appeal for tolerance is seen in such documents as the Apocalypse of John (for the first reaction) and the Apologies of writers such as Aristides and the author of *To Diognetus* for the second response. The last-named gives a most appealing description of how Christians understood their earthly citizenship while they firmly professed a heavenly loyalty. It is perhaps a tract that illustrates as clearly as could be done the teaching of Jesus in the Tribute Money story (Mark 12:13–17). Nonetheless such an appeal was not always successful, and the nicely balanced arrangement of a double allegiance, rendering to Caesar his due and to God his due, broke down under the church's refusal to surrender its political and social rights, and the Roman state's firm determination to secure cohesion within the empire by eliminating all types of activity thought to be subversive or bizarre or non-amenable to control.

With the coming to sole power of Constantine, following his victory over Licinius in AD 324, the era of active state persecution was at an end. Certain results followed, which are worth tabulating. They left a legacy that was carried forward to succeeding centuries, and may be said to be with us today.

1. The church now enjoyed the patronage of the state. Holy days became holidays; and at a different level the clergy were brought under civil control and given certain privileges and exemptions in matters like taxation.

2. Bishops became great persons at court, and the emperor received and treated them as important social and political figures. This attitude of respect for the church's leadership had a sting in its tail when the civil ruler claimed to be ex-officio chairman in ecclesiastical councils, and aspired to the right to give decisions in theological matters.

3. Not unnaturally clerical ambition crept in, as the emperor's favour was curried and his influence sought. It is easy to see how this state of affairs would lead to corruption and self-serving venality.

4. Being a Christian became both popular and socially advantageous in the community. The motives behind conversion to the faith were rendered doubtful, and the result which produced a church of professing, nominal adherents was nothing short of calamitous.

5. Indiscriminate baptism of infants to ensure their place in the visible church was wedded to a theological dogma of 'original guilt' found in Origen (AD 231) and developed especially in Augustine's time (AD 400 onwards).[8] Newly born infants were considered to be damned from birth – on the basis of a misreading of the Latin text of Romans 5:12 which was taken to read 'in Adam all sinned' – and so they needed the sacrament of baptismal remission to deal with their guilt and enable them to escape the pains of purgatorial limbo, should they die prematurely. The popular mind quickly associated infant baptism with a superstitious formula of inoculation against the evils of limbo; and the theology of initiation was debased into a priestly confidence trick.

This thumb-nail sketch of developments which followed the Constantinian 'settlement' will at least have shown how testy 'living in the world' became for Christians. The network of manifold problems remains with us.

Living in the World

Modern-day Christians trying to make sense of their calling in the complexity of contemporary society are often confused and bewildered. Have any guidelines emerged from our brief study?

We submit that there are three areas in which crucial matters may be thought through and decided upon.

a. First, any 'church' that would claim to be genetically connected with the New Testament models of Christianity should take seriously the *concern with discipline*. It is inescapable that our forebears had definite ideas about what constituted suitable moral attitudes for a professed disciple, and strove to enforce some disciplinary procedures. Paul has a sensitive and pastoral interest, and he reminds us that all discipline must be practised in the right spirit (in love) and for the right purpose (it should be remedial or at least salutary). Matthew's gospel (18:12–20) offers a kind of 'rule of discipline,' which gives evidence that it reflects a church situation including problems of erring members, church disputes, reconciliation and forgiveness, and united decisions touching the community. Incidental references such as Galatians 6:1; 1 Timothy 5:1; and James 5:16,19,20 agree, in spite of their various settings, on the need for considerateness and a tender, compassionate spirit; and the passages warn of a danger that our judgments may be overharsh so that we forget that we too are only human and frail. Jesus' words in Matthew 7:1–5 are directed to this reminder. But the verses equally insist on the need for congregational and personal life to be submitted to the judgment of the church and unworthy behaviour corrected (1 Cor. 6:1–8).

b. There is a *prophetic dimension* to the church's ministry that ensures its freedom to speak out against the evils of society and to offer independent counsel unfettered by political or bureaucratic control. To have the church function simply as a department of the state – a situation that prevailed in Henry VIII's time and lives on in some east European countries and to some extent in Israel today – under the aegis of 'a ministry of religious affairs,' is an intolerable situation, since its voice is then effectively silenced and its freedom to lead in matters of conscience is curtailed. This is a powerful argument for the separation of church and state, at least at the level where the church is free from all trammels that would prevent it from exercising its prophetic ministry as the state's conscience and critic. The state has its authority within the limits set by such teaching as Romans 13. But once it exceeds those limits and usurps a demonic or totalitarian role as in Revelation 13 there must be space for Christians to utter the protest: 'We must obey God, not men' (Acts 5:29; see Acts 4:19,20).[9]

c. Reducing the viable options to simplistic terms, we note three possibilities concerning *the church's attitude to the world*. There may be 'immersion in the world' as all lines of demarcation are rubbed out and the church loses its distinctive identity. There may be the opposite extreme, often found in such historical examples as parts of the monastic movement or attempts at setting up a theocracy or pietist enclave, of 'isolation from the world.' The New Testament gives no mandate for this kind of withdrawal which implies a fortress mentality; indeed Paul explicitly denies it in 1 Corinthians 5:10. Finally, there may be a stance of 'detachment from the world.' The last is really the only authentic Christian position that can claim scriptural precedent. This posture gives the church a unique function in society as a grouping that is friend to all who love liberty, oppose social injustice, and champion the rights of the oppressed, yet a group that reserves the right to act as social critic of current political and economic policies and the freedom to offer and implement proposals that are unpopular and run against the stream. Above all, the church is in the world as its 'salt' and 'light' (Matt. 5:13,14), and it is a challenging reminder to the men of this world that the 'world, as it is now, will not last much longer' (1 Cor. 7:31). It is wise political sense as well as basic theological truth to recall this and to live 'as though' (1 Cor. 7:30,31)[10] man's true destiny is not found in this interplay of political and social forces but in his healthy and responsible attitudes to God, his needy neighbour, and his true self (Luke 12:13–34).

9
Today's Church: Meaningful Models

A book published in 1960 carried a significant title, *Images of the Church in the New Testament*. The author, Paul S. Minear, provided a compendious list and discussed the many terms used in the New Testament to describe the church: its nature, character, function and destiny. Some of these descriptions are well-known: the Lord's body, building and bride are all found gathered in one New Testament letter, Ephesians. Other items in Minear's list are less obvious, such as the vine and the flock of God. Each term has something special to contribute to our understanding, and we need the wide variety of these many terms – Minear's count is upwards of one hundred – to portray the fulness of the church.

Our task in this concluding chapter is to ask which models are most relevant in today's world. But before we attempt an answer, it may be well to review some of the roles the church is thought to play in society. We are here looking at the church as a sociological entity, and enquiring how it functions as a need-fulfilling agency in the community.

The Church in Society

a. The standardized picture of the church in the Protestant and Reformed tradition is one which envisages the gathering of Christians *in a 'lecture room' setting*. The assembly of believers – for which good precedent may be found in Hebrews 10:25 (cf. Heb. 12:22,23)[1] – is arranged in seats that are so placed as to direct focal attention to the raised, central pulpit. There the minister is essentially 'a minister of the divine word,' charged to speak as he/she leads or directs the service in prayer or sermon. While several other ingredients in the worship are customary and much cherished, such as congregational singing and united praying, the main elements are the reading and expounding of scripture as God's word written. Again, there is ample precedent for this form of service, derived from both Old Testament examples (for instance, Ezra 10:9–17; Neh. 8:4 in the context of ch. 8:2–18 actually describes Ezra's platform as 'a pulpit made for the purpose,' RSV) and the post-exilic institution of the Jewish synagogue. Synagogue liturgy centres on the two parts of a reciting of various scriptural lections and a homily that seeks to apply those readings to the needs of the people. Good illustrations occur in Luke 4:16–30 and Acts 13:14–43.

This understanding of worship is determined, then, chiefly by the spoken and received 'word.' Calvin in one place uses the phrase, 'to go to the sermon,' *aller au sermon*, for attendance at Sunday worship, and this phrase exactly makes the point. Communication from God to man and man's response to the divine are in terms of the verbal medium. 'Hear the word of the Lord' is the summons which is also a gracious invitation. 'Pay attention to *what* you hear' (Mark 4:24), which is handed down in the Lukan version as 'Be careful, then, *how* you listen' (Luke 8:18) sums up the genius of this type of worship practice. Words are spoken on the authority of the 'word inscripturated,' and the worshipping company responds with its verbal assent as a token that it has 'understood' the implications of all that the worship seeks to enforce.

There is obviously great value in this model, and it has nourished and sustained the life of God's people from apostolic days (Acts 20:7–12) and sub-apostolic times (as in Justin's description of divine service in Rome around AD 150), through the era of great preachers like Ambrose and Chrysostom to the Reformation church period and the Puritan divines, on to such eminent exponents of 'the centrality of the sermon' as Jonathan Edwards, F. W. Robertson, Joseph Parker, C. H. Spurgeon and D. M. Lloyd-Jones.

Nonetheless it is not difficult to detect some flaws in this pattern of worship, which are only too evident in our day and have created a backlash of contemporary distaste for listening to sermons. The barrage of words, spoken by a single individual who holds a central, elevated position 'six feet above contradiction' is resisted by the audience who find it difficult to have their attention held as long as they play the role of passive auditors. The sermon has traditionally contained a high intellectual content to be grasped by people who are used to thinking in abstract or highly noetic terms. The artisan, homemaker and factory worker are bidden to enter a world quite different from the one in which they exercise their daily skills; and it is small wonder that the sermon fails to impact on their life and they quickly tire of 'being spoken to.' Educationally there is a serious objection to the principle that underlies the classic theory of the sermon, namely that 'teaching is by talking and learning is by listening.'

There is an unmistakable – indeed an indispensable – place for the sermon, but it cannot be given the monopoly of worship; nor can the image of the church as a school, patterned on the Jewish synagogue called a 'house of instruction' be regarded as the exclusive and sole model today, even if we concede the importance of preaching as the conveyance of God's will in his word, both read and proclaimed.

b. The Catholic model makes its appeal to visually observed action and movement; it may be called in simplistic yet non-derogatory terms *the model of the theatre.* The chief emphasis falls on the dramatic elements in the high moments of worship, especially the elevation of the host in the service of the mass. But other features are equally calculated to register an impression on the eye of the beholder.

The priest is dressed in vestments, with colours appropriate to each church season. Light and shade are skilfully employed as an aid to worship, since aesthetic experience is believed to have much to contribute to worship. Pictures, candles, icons and especially the crucifix are pressed into service as vehicles through which the later church sought to enrich its 'cult.' It broke away decisively from the Jewish model on the issue of there being no visible representation of the divine; the examples of pagan art in the synagogues of Galilee and the dispersion were later denounced by the rabbis.[2] The evidence shows that Christians were just as reluctant to give a pictorial representation to the crucified form of Jesus, and only later resorted to the image of the crucifix.[3] But once the figure of the crucified as a symbol established itself, it caught on and the plain cross became gilded with ornate embellishments and eventually led to the cult of the 'sacred heart' of Jesus, and his human mother Mary.

Catholic worship seeks deliberately to create an atmosphere by such features in the service as choral singing, constant movement in procession, genuflexion and gesticulations (in charismatic settings) as well as bell-ringing and incense-offering in the more traditional modes. The focal point is determined by the altar, even when the altar is relocated from the apse of the basilica and situated in a central position around which the worshippers gather. The role of bishop and priest as officiants at the altar is central within this focus, and it is their actions in word and deed that climax the eucharistic drama. The medium is the 'eyegate,' and it is fatally easy for the worshippers in the nave of the church to be detached as simple spectators of what is being done in their name at the high altar.

The psychological appeal in this concept of worship is very obvious. Most people are attracted by warm, living colours; their aesthetic taste is both aroused and satisfied by beauty in works of sculpture, pictures and frescoes, and religious objects of devotion; their attention is kept alive by a constant flow of movement and drama, exploiting the appeal of body language, while the set form of the liturgy with choral music creates a sense of otherworldliness and fascination with the divine which Otto has taught us to call the numinous.

But attractiveness and aestheticism can be secured at a high price. In this instance, the detachment of the worshipper from all that is being done is regrettable; and while the reforms following Vatican II have done much to make the liturgy intelligible by recasting it in the vernacular, and have eagerly sought for congregational participation in scripture study and eucharist, priestly ministrations still drive a wedge between God and the individual worshipper, as is clear from the basic theology of the mass itself as a priest-oriented function.

Much has been achieved, since the Vatican Council which led to the papal promulgation of the *Constitution on the*

Sacred Liturgy in December 1963, to encourage Catholics to share more fully in the central service of the church's life and worship. 'The full and active participation by all the people is the aim to be considered before all else'[4] sets out a laudable goal that the revised theology and practice of the mass sought to attain. The upshot was that the traditional Latin service was replaced at a single stroke by a much simplified and more comprehensible service, recited in the living language of the people, with four possible canons of the mass, i.e. the great eucharistic prayer, and the service was brought into the midst of the congregation. The use of an altar table that is freestanding ensured that 'the priest can walk all around it and can celebrate facing the people.' Nonetheless 'it should be in a position such that the entire congregation will naturally focus their attention on it.' Other revisions were no less noteworthy, including the prominence given to the scripture and its exposition, the curtailing of the number of images 'lest they distract the people's attention from the ceremonies,' and the congregational sharing in prayers and singing. These reforms have certainly contributed to a fresh perception of the mass that is no longer 'an external spectacle, a kind of "tableau vivant" played before an audience which took virtually no part.'[5] The day of 'mumbled masses, stiff with formalism, perfunctorily performed, and celebrated as if the congregation did not exist'[6] has passed, bringing in its place a new sense of liberation and relief.

Simpler, more modest church furnishings and a more humanized type of worship have led to a re-emphasis on God's immanence, his presence with his people as distinct from a presence that is remote and forbidding. The theological shift is seen in the move away from the mass as a propitiatory sacrifice to a recovery of the service as a celebration of joy in the risen Lord. Nevertheless the eucharistic sacrifice is still regarded as a perpetuating of the offering of Christ on the cross, and merit theology lingers on in the section of the missal that treats of indulgences, expiation, the 'treasury of the church' and purgatory. It is then not surprising that, with all the far-ranging liberalizing reforms and the radical overhaul of the Catholic mass, it is still claimed that Christ's presence in the sacrifice of the mass is tied to the 'person of the minister' and 'the eucharistic species;' and 'it is indeed the priest alone, who, acting in the person of Christ, consecrates the bread and wine.' At the same time more openness is given to the presence of Christ in his church and 'the role of the faithful' is granted to share personally in the eucharistic sacrifice.

The Vatican II documents express caution in the matter of the veneration of relics and icons. Pictorial representations of God, Christ, Mary and the saints may be helpful – according to personal taste. The role accorded Mary in Christian devotion following the Catholic tradition has recently come to prominence, and deserves a comment.

Scholarly interpretation of Mary's place in scripture and early Christianity is a rewarding exercise; and it is generally conceded that her role as co-redemptrix or mediatrix between God and Jesus in popular Catholicism[7] rests on no secure exegetical base. The 'quest of the historical Mary' hardly justifies the role claimed for her in Marian devotion. The most that a trajectory through early Christianity reveals is the way she became increasingly 'idealized' as a model believer. The symbol of Mary as 'daughter of Zion' and the new Eve belongs to a post-canonical period.

Small groups in the charismatic tradition have seen Catholics and non-Catholics brought together in free association. The invoking of Mary in prayer has been one feature of this enterprise; and it is openly granted that 'a living perception and recognition of the role of Mary is particularly important in a movement such as the Charismatic Renewal.'[8] Part of the reason for this claim is the need to supply the maternal image in God's character. Part of the justification is the typecasting of Mary as a pentecostal believer in the lifetime of Jesus.[9] And yet another facet which can only be regarded with some suspicion is the view that sees her as an active agent in human redemption. 'She mediated the Holy Spirit to others and she continues to be a presence to all who ask her to come into their lives and allow the Holy Spirit to lead them as she was led by Him.'[10]

The claims registered by Suenens, 'We breathe in Mary and breathe out the Spirit,' or Maloney, 'A charismatic Christian who wants to be full of the Holy Spirit . . . will find

Mary one of the greatest helps in this growth,'[11] are so open
to misunderstanding as to be dangerous and detrimental to
a faithful understanding of the nature of New Testament
Christianity.[12]

At base it is debatable whether an approach to God with
undue emphasis on the visible and evidential is a real service
to the gospel. Such a way of worship fails to assert, as should
be done, the nature of faith as trust in God's promises. It
even destroys the confidence that underlies all true worship,
that God in Jesus Christ – and him crucified, risen and
glorified – has done everything required for human salvation.
Worship 'in spirit and in reality' (John 4:23,24) must be both
a necessary conviction underlying divine service and a controlling factor in all that is said and done.

c. Attempts to relate the church directly to the modern
world and to give it a streamlined image find their most
blatant expression when business methods and techniques are
called in to promote its function in the community. What
results is the characterization of the church *as a corporation*.
The model is one of the Christian society as a community
service agency, offering a commodity ('religion' or 'the
Christian faith') in an attractive package. The church is
thought of as functioning within the secular world to retail
religion, and the methods pressed into service are lifted
directly from the techniques of merchandising and selling.
The various approaches to successful business are taken over.

First the needs of the community are analysed and collated.
Where a spiritual 'need' is weak or dormant, efforts are made
to stimulate it and to arouse public interest. Then, sustained
and appealing advertising holds the church's image before the
community's eye; and the interest of the neighbourhood or
area is awakened. This is followed by a packaging of the
church's message to show its relevance and adequacy to meet
human needs. The enterprise is backed by ongoing service to
the community and a penetration of business groups, local
civic organizations, schools and colleges, and political structures. Inevitably methods that produce 'results' in terms of
accessions to church membership rolls, increased cash flow
to church budgets and enhanced popularity as a public image,

are credited with success. Conversely, methods that do not yield quantifiable results are written off as valueless.

Even if the above paragraph may be discounted as something of a caricature of local churches in general, it still remains uncomfortably true that some, if not all, of these features are seen in some large American churches and in large-scale evangelistic endeavours. With the implicit slogan, 'Nothing succeeds like success,' this understanding of the church's role in society is oriented to growth and influence that is statistically measurable; and no effort is spared to present – and to exploit – the gospel's appeal. Enthusiasm and dedication and drive are among the most laudable components of this activity; and faced with mounting secularism in society and much apathy in an unco-ordinated church life, this operation may claim to be justified by its results seen in outwardly impressive churches and teeming congregations who are sufficiently 'alive' as to produce astronomical giving in their stewardship and an infectious concern to see their church 'grow.'

Once again, gains are offset by some serious weaknesses.[13] Business methods can be a corrosive force tending to distort and destroy the very commodity it seeks to promote. 'Needs' can be artificially created and shamelessly exploited, and human personality gets bruised and fractured in the process. Statistics may tell only part of the story – sometimes indeed they can distract the church from its real mission which requires fidelity even where God withholds 'success' (1 Cor. 4:2). Programmes organized to make the outsider aware of the church can outlive their usefulness and become ends in themselves. A 'popular' church is beset with an immediate danger of betraying its Lord who was 'despised and rejected by men.' And with all the concern for numerical growth, it can be forgotten that God alone gives the increase (1 Cor. 3:6).

d. Another style of church life, well-known in our time, centres on the need for 'fellowship.' We have already seen how vital a part this term plays in New Testament Christianity; it became apparent in our survey that the biblical emphasis falls rather on the objective realities that unite believers than on their personal feelings of warmth and mutual regard. In the type of churchly image we are now considering this emphasis is reversed. 'Fellowship' is understood as together-ness, contact and mutual support among the adherents of a local congregation.

In latter-day Christianity a theology of the church and its message has developed on this basis. It insists that what the church exists for is to meet the gregarious instinctual needs of men and women, to make them 'feel good' or 'feel accepted' by relating them to their fellow human beings. This is the essence of relational theology that expounds the biblical message in terms of its answer to the human predicament of alienation, isolation, frustration and a sense of being deprived of that warm, accepting friendship which is God's offer in Christ and his people. The most worthy exponents of relational theology integrate the human situation with the preaching of divine grace and forgiveness. Justification by faith is restyled in terms of acceptance by God who meets us at our levels of despair and self-abnegation, and promises a fresh beginning by a new relationship with himself. But it is possible for relational theology to degenerate into a humanistic ploy of proffered self-help and psychological counselling. Then the gospel message is attenuated into an invitation to ways of relating to other people and of facing the stresses and strains of modern living. When this happens, the church itself becomes little better than a society of mutual sharing and caring (which, to be sure, are valuable assets) and its image and role are those of a *social club*.

An associated danger is that a 'club mentality' tends to produce exclusivistic attitudes as members are drawn to others of similar disposition and bent. Even sharing experiences may become unhealthy if it creates inter-dependence within the group, and the fulness of the church's life is impaired by the fostering of special groups with a separatist tendency and alienated from the life of the community as a whole. The clique within the church is a danger as old and prevalent as the Corinthian situation; and it is equally open to apostolic rebuke (1 Cor. 1:10–13, 3:3–5).

True, the same apostle continues by elaborating his teaching on the inter-relatedness of the body (1 Cor. 12), but Paul never concedes that each member can live in isolation, whether singly or in a group. The trouble, it seems, with the type of church life and worship that chooses catering for human needs as its aim is that it downplays the corporate life in which all Christians share, and tends to lose the outward-looking aspects of the church in evangelism and service to the community at large.

Summing Up

In retrospect it appears that each model has some important elements to make it appealing and necessary; yet there are equally obvious deficiencies that require scrutiny and amendment, especially when ideas and emphases are taken to excess. The Protestant concentration on the divine word needs a counterbalancing stress on the worship of God in the beauty of his holiness. The highly sophisticated techniques of business management when applied to the church's outreach must be supplemented with the emphasis on the value of the individual and his sub-surface needs that a kind of relational theology may offer.

Conversely, the magic of colour and movement in Catholic worship requires the reinforcing of some authoritative word spoken to man's mind to interpret the ritual lest it lapse into superstition without cognitive meaning. The same divine word of truth is the 'given' element to test all criteria of success and to come to the rescue of a relational theology that has only subjective self-help to offer. Yet the proclamation of the age-old word in scripture and sacrament, with its reassuring comfort in notes of free grace and dying love, needs to be grounded in the present needs of the people and related to living the Christian life in the tumult and strain of our modern days.

Images in the Scripture

In other words, whatever model happens to fit in any particular social setting, the need remains for that model to be evaluated and corrected by referring to the form of the church viewed in its scriptural matrix.

Three biblical images predominate. Since we have considered them in the previous chapters, only a minimum of comment is needed here. At this point, we rehearse them in bold outline, and ask once again: What is the meaningful model of the church for today's world?

a. The Temple of the Lord

This familiar title, with its roots in the Old Testament-Jewish heritage of the church, is used to great effect by the main New Testament writers.[14] Paul employs both an individualistic (1 Cor. 6:19) and a corporate (1 Cor. 3:16,17) dimension in his appeal. He shows how the Corinthians should revere the habitation of the Holy Spirit, which is both the believer's person-as-a-body and the congregation-as-an-entity.

Peter (1 Pet. 2:5) relates the idea to worship in the spiritual temple where 'spiritual and acceptable sacrifices [are offered] to God through Jesus Christ.' The letter to the Hebrews (9:23–28) describes the heavenly temple where Christ's perfect sacrifice was made with eternal, unrepeatable consequences. In the Revelation, perfect worship is offered in the new temple which is no material creation but the visible, glorious presence of God himself (Rev. 21:22) whose throne is over all (Rev. 22:3*b*).

The uniting feature in all these figures is the call and claim of worship, addressed by the church to the holy God who is worthy of praise, adoration and devotion in himself and also because of his mighty acts in creation (Rev. 4:11) and redemption (Rev. 5:11–14). This may be termed the chief theme of both Testaments as the revelation of God in his created world and in his covenant of grace evokes the wondering gratitude of his people (Deut. 26:5–11; Eph. 1:3–14).

The church's priority is hereby set for all time. Psalm 96 rings out the call to ascribe to the Lord the glory due to his name, to bring an offering of praise and to enter his courts. There can be no going back on this prior claim, no substitute for what is the church's ultimate agenda and raison d'être. It is in the world *to facilitate the worship of God*, and to remind the men and women of this age of the powers of the coming age that already are pressing in upon them as they unite with the heavenly host and the saints triumphant (Heb. 12:22–24; it is the theme of Ephesians and the Revelation).

b. The Body of Christ

Again, this is a well-known picture drawn from 1 Corinthians 12:12–27; Romans 12:4,5; Ephesians 1:23, 4:4,12,16, 5:23,30. Christ is or is like the head, with the church as his complementary body. From that analogy Paul works out the thesis that the church is (a) subject to its directing head, for he is its origin – a play on words possible from the Hebrew *rosh* which can have either meaning; and (b) made up of diverse yet inter-related parts. Each member has a part to play – again we may detect a play on the word 'member' which can refer both to physical parts of the human anatomy (as in Col. 3:5) and to church members (as in 1 Cor. 12:27).

The thrust of these passages is one of activity. Christ directs, controls and energizes the members (albeit through the 'ligaments' of Eph. 4:16) so that they may serve his purpose in the world. Thus part of the church's reason for being is that *it may minister to the world as Christ's agent.*

c. The Family of God

In our final section we suggest that this image goes even deeper than the two designations just treated. We are particularly concerned to propose a symbol of church life that will have immediate and intelligible appeal, and prepare the ground for a later understanding of the role of new Christians as worshippers in the temple of the Lord and workers in the body of Christ. Before these high privileges and necessary responsibilities are considered, it may be helpful to recall a more easily understood sense of *belonging to the divine family.*

Ephesians 2:19 affirms the new place of Gentiles as 'members of the family of God,' while a later verse (Eph. 3:14,15) sets the family-idea on a firm base of the divine Fatherhood, portraying God as the archetype of every kind of family, whether angelic or human. Thus we touch here on an elemental human relationship: we all exist as part of an earthly family – even social outcasts once had a human parent! And we are related to our fellows since there is one God, the

Creator, who claims the allegiance of his creatures as potential sons and daughters. The Pauline statement in Acts 17:28 goes further: 'We too are his children.' The image of God, although defaced and deformed, is there in all God's human creatures. That 'image' rests like a suspended nimbus above every member of our race, recalling what man was destined to be and may become in Jesus Christ whose characteristic name for God is *Abba*, dear Father.

In the family mutual relationships are inescapable. This truth derives from the Genesis creation accounts (Gen. 1:27,28, 2:18–24) and is reinforced in the summary statement of what is meant by 'Adam' (=humankind: Gen. 5:1,2). The same inescapable inter-relatedness of life runs through scripture's story (for example, Ps. 68:5,6) to the teaching of Jesus and the ecclesiology of the epistles (Mark 10:2–12 and parallels; Rom. 14:7–9; Eph. 4:25). The church at its best reflects all that is noblest and most worthwhile in human family life: attitudes of caring and mutual regard; understanding of needs, whether physical or of the spirit; and above all the sense of 'belonging' to a social unit in which we find acceptance without pretence or make-believe. Home life is for many people a sphere where they can be 'natural' as themselves. God's house shares this character when its worship and fellowship create an atmosphere in which there is free expression of our true selves, always in the hope that we can learn from one another and mature as we grow into our Elder Brother's likeness (Rom. 8:29; Eph. 4:13–15).

Meal times in family life are precious moments, more especially to be valued when the family is dispersed for eight or ten hours of the working day. It cannot be accidental that Old Testament theophanies and New Testament appearances of the risen Christ are set at a meal table (Gen. 18:1–15; Judges 13:9–20; Luke 24; John 21; Acts 1:4, RSV marg., 10:41). The Lord's table remains for the Christian-in-the-family the high point of revelation and communion. There the Lord is present, as 'host and sacrifice' but always in his living power and grace that point back to his finished atonement. There believers sit in union with one another as family members around a common table. There the fellowship of the saints unites the church in heaven with the 'militant company on earth'. There we anticipate the day of the final homecoming of all God's people, and the cry of 'Our Lord, come' (1 Cor. 16:22; *Didache* 10:6) looks ahead to the greater festival and nobler celebration when the church will be perfected in God's plan for a restored universe (Eph. 1:10) of which the church is at present, however imperfectly and obscurely, a growing microcosm. But it will one day take its final shape as 'the church . . . in all its beauty, pure and faultless, without spot or wrinkle, or any other imperfection' (Eph. 5:27). And the context of Ephesians 5 encourages us to believe that then God's original design for the family of humankind will be gloriously achieved as the 'time comes for all things to be made new' (Acts 3:21; Rev. 21:5).

Notes

Chapter One

[1] E. Brunner, *Man in Revolt*, E.T. 1939, pp. 96–99, uses the word *Ansprechbarkeit*, man's 'answerability' or 'addressability' – the responsible awareness which is his as God's gift in grace.

[2] H. R. Mackintosh, *The Christian Experience of Forgiveness*, 1927, p. 241.

[3] J. S. Whale, *Christian Doctrine*, 1941, p. 124.

[4] G. W. H. Lampe, *God as Spirit*, 1977, p. 177. So too A. Schlatter, *Gottes Gerechtigkeit:* Ein Kommentar zum Römerbrief, 1935, p. 315: 'A man cannot become a believer in solitude. He can become one only through fellowship with those who speak the word of faith to him. . . . For the word is the message of the Christ who calls him into the church.' Compare 1 Corinthians 3:5.

[5] J. Calvin, *Institutes of the Christian Religion*, 4.1.4, 10.

[6] In his *The Quest of the Historical Jesus*, E.T. 1910.

[7] A judicious discussion of the role of Peter in the New Testament church and its relation to disciplinary procedures especially in Matthew is given in *Peter in the New Testament*, 1973, edd. R. E. Brown, K. P. Donfried and J. Reumann especially pp. 91–107.

[8] A. M. Hunter, *The Unity of the New Testament*, 1946, ch. 6; R. Newton Flew, *Jesus and His Church*, 1943.

[9] W. Manson, *Jesus the Messiah*, 1943, p. 185 quotes the lines of Horatius Bonar's hymn:
> 'The Kingdom that I seek
> Is Thine, so let the way
> That leads to it be Thine.'

Chapter Two

[1] 'Ecclesia, the Church, must, I suggest, be retained for the society which knew the difference made by the Resurrection.' This sentence stands as the conclusion of G. Johnston's excellent discussion, *The Doctrine of the Church in the New Testament*, 1943, p. 52.

[2] I. H. Marshall, 'The Significance of Pentecost,' *Scottish Journal*

of Theology 30, 1977, pp. 347–369.

[3] R. P. Ehlinger, 'Le récit de la première Pentecôte chrétienne,' *Bible et Terre Sainte* 11, 1958, p. 5, writes on Acts 2:2–4: 'This most suggestive description of the remarkable outpouring of the Spirit is less precise than appears at first reading. It is artistically composed of imaginative themes and comparisons, "as of a wind . . . as of fire." Such themes suggest an atmosphere of religious reflection.'

[4] K. Stendahl, *Paul Among Jews and Gentiles*, 1976, p. 118.

[5] Later Christian writers, listed in R. P. Dalmais' article, 'La sainte Sion, mère de toutes les églises,' *Bible et Terre Sainte* 11, 1958, pp. 3–5, refer to the location of the Jerusalem church in terms that speak of 'holy Sion' (*sancta Sion*), the mother of all churches (*mater omnium ecclesiarum*). By the time of the emperor Hadrian (AD 130) there was a 'small church of God' in Epiphanius' words (*Weights and Measures* 14), and 'seven synagogues' on mount Zion that possibly may have been Jewish-Christian churches (J. Finegan, *The Archeology of the New Testament*, 1969, p. 150).

[6] The historical and theological factors that led to a widening of the gulf between synagogue and church are described by Jacob Jocz, *The Jewish People and Jesus Christ*, 1954, pp. 42–65. He lists the following items that led to a hardening Jewish reaction to the Hebrew Christians:

(1) active persecution which was directed against them in the form of social ostracism, religious excommunication and suppression; (2) liturgical alterations made to the Jewish worship, as stress was laid on the absolute unity of God and as the Decalogue was omitted in the daily service lest the impression be given the commandments had greater importance than the rest of Moses' law; (3) the introduction of a prayer (made not long after the fall of Jerusalem) cursing 'the heretics,' i.e. Hebrew Christians who were worshipping cryptically and who would be exposed and isolated by their refusing to pray, 'And for slanderers let there by no hope . . . and may Nazoreans and heretics (*minim*) perish as in a moment and be blotted out from the book of life'; and (4) calumniations of the person of Jesus, in particular that he was born illegitimately, became a magician, led Israel astray, and died a shameful death.

[7] The allegation that Luke's story of a mass conversion and subsequent baptism of three thousand persons in Jerusalem is 'quite a trick' and 'nothing short of a miracle' in Jerusalem at the height of the dry season (R. Zehnle, *The Making of the Church*, 1969, pp. 6,7) and so unhistorical may be countered by two pieces of recent archaeological evidence. Jewish ritual immersion pools or *mikva'oth* have been unearthed by B. Mazar just south of the Temple mount; these may have been used for self-administered baptisms before apostolic witnesses as in the practice of proselyte baptism. Then, on Mount Zion near to the traditional site of the first Judaeo-Christian community, what are claimed as Essene

pools have been discovered and identified by B. Pixner as part of an Essene 'camp' near the 'gate of the Essenes' (Josephus, *Jewish War*, 5.145). This would provide even more accessible facilities for mass immersions, as recorded in Acts 2. See the reports in *Christian News from Israel* 26, 1976, pp. 12–14,53,54.

[8] B. Reicke, *Diakonie, Festfreude und Zelos in Verbindung mit der altchristlichen Agapenfeier*, 1951, pp. 25–28.

[9] See G. N. Stanton, *Jesus of Nazareth in New Testament Preaching*, 1974, ch. 1.

[10] E. L. Mascall, *The Importance of Being Human*, 1959, p. 83, describes the fall of the first human pair in this way: 'Like a microscopic crack in a china vase, it initiated a process of disintegration and corruption whose consequences spread far beyond the area of their origin and affected the whole subsequent history of the human race and of the material realm.'

Chapter Three

[1] The three most helpful treatments of the term *koinōnia* = fellowship and other possible translations are: A. R. George, *Communion with God in the New Testament*, 1953; J. G. Davies, *Members One of Another*, 1958; and J. M. McDermott, 'The Biblical Doctrine of KOINONIA,' *Biblische Zeitschrift*, new series 19, 1975, pp. 64–77, 219–233.

[2] McDermott, pp. 232f.

[3] George, p. 1.

[4] E. B. Allo, *La première épître aux Corinthiens*, 1934, p.5.

[5] See P. T. O'Brien, 'The Fellowship Theme in Philippians,' *Reformed Theological Review* 37, 1978, pp. 9–18.

[6] F. Hauck in *TDNT* vol. 3, p. 805.

[7] C. K. Barrett, *The Second Epistle of Paul to the Corinthians*, 1973, p. 241.

[8] McDermott, p. 225.

[9] George, pp. 133, 184f.

Chapter Four

[1] J. V. Taylor, *The Go-Between God*, 1972.

[2] Book of Common Catechism.

[3] See Arnold Bittlinger, *Gifts and Graces*, 1967; David L. Baker, 'The Interpretation of 1 Corinthians 12–14', *Evangelical Quarterly*, 46, 1974, pp. 224–234; John Goldingay, *The Church and the Gifts of the Spirit*, 1972.

[4] This, to be sure, is only one of several possible interpretations of the situation underlying 1 Corinthians 12:1–3. A recent alternative view is presented by W. C. van Unnik, 'Jesus: Anathema or Kyrios (1 Cor. 12:3)', *Christ and Spirit in the New Testament. In Honour of C. F. D. Moule*, edd. B. Lindars and S. S. Smalley,

1973, pp. 113–126. He wants to see the statement 'Jesus is accursed' as an incomplete but Christian utterance, faulted only by an intention to stay at the cross where Jesus 'became a curse' (Gal. 3:13; Deut. 21:23) and refusing to go on to include the resurrection when he was exalted as Lord (the second member of the confession in verse 3). But this interpretation fails to explain how Paul categorically denies that the statement 'Jesus is accursed' is ever inspired by the Spirit, whether incomplete or not.

^{5} These paragraphs submit the thesis that the key to an understanding of the spiritual gifts in 1 Corinthians 12–14 is to be found in Paul's defence of his ministry in 2 Corinthians 10–13. This view of what was at stake in Paul's debate with his detractors at Corinth owes much to H. D. Betz's exposition, *Der Apostel Paulus und die sokratische Tradition*, 1972, especially pp. 132–137. He (rightly in my judgment) makes the central issue the setting of 2 Corinthians 12:19, 13:3–6 from which he concludes that the root problem at Corinth was one of 'what is the true evidence of the Christian apostle?' (p. 133). The two 'evidences' Paul appeals to are: (1) Paul's 'weakness' which is sustained in all crises by Christ's power living in him and (2) his concern for the upbuilding of all Christians at Corinth, which is the sign that authenticates his ministry (pp. 99,100). A third 'evidence' is Paul's own character as 'bold yet meek' (10:1) which reflects Christ's own power-in-weakness (13:4), just as Paul's unimpressive preaching – by worldly standards – reflects 'the word of the cross' (2 Cor. 10:10; 1 Cor. 1:18). As much as his apostolic status, it is Paul's person as a Christian that is being attacked, and what is at stake is the true definition of the Christian life.

^{6} K. Stendahl gives a generous assessment: 'It is not a question of whether glossolalia is a theologically proper phenomenon – of course it is. It is rather a question of how this phenomenon can be a force to the benefit of the whole church' (*Paul Among Jews and Gentiles*, p. 124). He adds a caution regarding a necessary criterion of all spiritual gifts: 'Not the gift that God gave, but God who gave the gift. The charismatics are in danger of becoming fascinated by the gift.'

^{7} The later restrictions placed on a woman's role in exercising the *charisma* of prophecy (in 1 Tim. 2:11–15) may reflect an attempt to correct some abuses that stem from an over-zealous application of the Pauline egalitarian charter of Galatians 3:28. Signs of how excesses may have followed are seen at Corinth where there were enthusiastic and pneumatic forms of worship in which men and women mixed together in a way seeming to resemble the cult of Dionysus.

For an interesting study of the way later corrections were supplied to Paul's teaching to meet pressing needs, see J. E. Crouch, *The Origin and Intention of the Colossian Haustafel*, 1972, especially pp. 141–145,151; cf. *The New International Dictionary of*

NT Theology, ed. C. Brown, vol. 3, 1978, pp. 928–32.

Chapter Five

[1] See *Peter in the New Testament*, 1973, edd. R. E. Brown, K. P. Donfried and J. Reumann which updates the discussion in J. Lowe, *Saint Peter*, 1956, and O. Cullmann, *Peter: Disciple, Apostle, Martyr*, second edition, 1962.

[2] J. Jeremias, *TDNT* vol. 3, p. 752.

[3] O. Cullmann, *TDNT* vol. 6, p. 108.

[4] The debate between Sohm and Harnack who argued over whether the church was organized from the start is covered in W. D. Davies, *Christian Origins and Judaism*, 1962, 'A Normative Pattern of Church life in the New Testament,' pp. 199–229.

[5] We should also include Gaius, Quartus and perhaps Erastus, referred to in Romans 16:23. See H. J. Cadbury, 'Erastus of Corinth,' *Journal of Biblical Literature*, 50, 1931, pp. 42–58.

[6] See 'Comment on Ephesians 2:20,' pp. 72–75.

[7] This is the customary interpretation, opposed – not very convincingly – by E. Best, 'Bishops and Deacons: Philippians 1, 1,' *Studia Evangelica*, 4, 1968, pp. 371–76, who thinks that Paul is being mildly ironical and downplays these self-chosen titles at Philippi.

[8] For the prophet as exercising a ministry of pastoral teaching see David Hill, *New Testament Prophecy*, 1979. See too his earlier essay, 'Christian Prophets as Teachers or Instructors in the Church,' in *Prophetic Vocation in the New Testament and Today*, ed. J. Panagopoulos, 1977, pp. 108–130.

[9] K. H. Rengstorf, *TDNT* vol. 2, p. 158.

[10] This feature may be added to Hill's discussion of criteria used to test the prophetic claims in the early church. The community was called to 'judge' (1 Cor. 14:29) and to note the effects of his word on the life of the community, specifically whether the prophet built up the church (1 Cor. 14:3,4,21), article quoted, p. 130. There is also the self-control of the prophets required in 1 Cor. 14:32 – for lack of which the Montanists were condemned (Eusebius, *Church History* 5.16.7–10; 5.17.2–4).

[11] See for the following B. H. Streeter, *The Primitive Church*, 1929.

[12] Notice the inserting of this word '*true* apostle' in 2 Corinthians 12:12 (in RSV); it is not represented in the Greek.

[13] This designation is accepted by those, such as G. W. Barker, W. L. Lane and J. R. Michaels, *The New Testament Speaks*, 1969, pp. 235–47, who uphold the authenticity of the letters as Paul's own composition.

[14] D. J. Harrington, 'The "Early Catholic" Writings of the New Testament: the Church Adjusting to World-History,' *The Word in the World*. Essays in honor of F. L. Moriarty, S. J., edd. R. J.

Clifford and G. W. MacRae, 1973, pp. 97–113.

[15] The Greek term is *haphai* (plural) from a verb 'to touch, make contact' and so 'to connect' whether in medical terms or other.

[16] Ph. Vielhauer, *Oikodome. Das Bild vom Bau in der christlichen Literatur vom NT bis Clemens Alexandrinus*, 1939, p. 140. Similarly 'both are picture-terms for one and the same reality of salvation' (Fr. Mussner, *Christus des Alls und die Kirche*, 1955, p. 111).

[17] We accept the conclusions of scholars following Streeter (*The Primitive Church*, pp. 74f., 82f.) that there was diversity in the early churches, corresponding to their geographical, cultural and theological setting, that only later tended to a uniform model of Christian institutions and ministry. Streeter offered this application of his theses:

> The Episcopalian, the Presbyterian, and the Independent can each discover the prototype of the system to which he himself adheres.

Illustrating from Lewis Carroll's *Alice* he quoted the Dodo at the end of the caucus race: 'Everyone has won, and all shall (sic: he meant 'must') have prizes' (p. ix).

An impressive body of opinion follows this conclusion which needs only the caution of W. D. Davies, 'Normative Pattern,' pp. 228, 229, that there are also criteria to guide and correct patterns of church life that seek to express the gospel.

Chapter Six

[1] The description of Christ as 'bridegroom' is often wrongly sentimentalized. One of its main emphases is the assertion of his lordship over his bride, the church, See R. A. Batey, *New Testament Nuptial Imagery*, 1971, pp. 67,68.

[2] Proclamation is thus nothing less than 'God's instrument,' as J. Murphy-O'Connor makes clear (*Paul on Preaching*, ch. 2).

[3] E. A. Speiser, *Genesis* (The Anchor Bible, 1964), pp. 217, 218.

[4] G. E. Ladd, 'The Parable of the Sheep and the Goats in Recent Interpretation,' *New Dimensions in NT Study*, edd. R. N. Longenecker and M. C. Tenney, 1974, pp. 191–99; J. Moltmann, *The Church in the Power of the Spirit*, 1977, pp. 126–130, under the heading 'Christ's Presence in the Poor.'

[5] The wearing of sandals was a privilege of free men. See J. Jeremias' comment on Luke 15:22 (*The Parables of Jesus*, 1963, p. 130).

[6] 'What a good story it is! at once vivid in what is recounted and skilful in what it leaves untold' (G. F. Nuttall, *The Moment of Recognition: Luke as Story-Teller*, 1978, pp. 3,4).

[7] Whether Qubeibeh or Abu Ghosh, suggested in view of the

appropriate mileage from Jerusalem (Luke 24:13). Imwas-Latrun is a site identified with Emmaus since the fourth century but the distance of 19 or more miles almost rules it out. Motza is the right distance, and there is some evidence that the name is concealed in Ammaus, a village known to Josephus (*Jewish War* 7.217). See J. Wilkinson, *Jerusalem as Jesus Knew It*, 1978, pp. 162–164.

[8] Reformed Catholicism in the post Vatican II period has departed from this idea. 'When the action of Christ is re-enacted, it is not important to repeat his words exactly. The Lord did not leave us a sort of magical formula' (*A New Catechism*, 1970, p. 333).

[9] C. J. Cadoux, 'Zwingli' in *Christian Worship*, ed. N. Micklem, 1936, p. 148. For the evidence of the eucharistic debates among the reformers see G. W. Bromiley, *Historical Theology. An Introduction*, 1978, ch. 20.

[10] Cadoux, p. 151.

[11] Cadoux, p. 148.

[12] Hence Calvin's insistence on 'efficacious signs' (*signa efficacia*) as distinct from Zwingli's description of 'bare signs' (*nuda signa*) i.e. substitutes for what is absent. Recent Roman and Anglican eucharistic theology is exploiting this teaching on effective signs in a doctrine of 'transignification.' See H. E. W. Turner in *Thinking about the Eucharist*. Essays by members of the Archbishops' Commission on Christian Doctrine, 1972, pp. 99–114.

[13] John Betjeman, 'Christmas.'

Chapter Seven

[1] E. Käsemann's title for his interpretation of the Fourth gospel, translated as *The Testament of Jesus*. A Study of the Gospel of John in the Light of Chapter 17, 1968.

[2] Of the Last Discourse as Jesus' testament R. E. Brown writes that the words 'are directed to Christians of all times' (*The Gospel According to John*, Anchor Bible, vol. 2, 1970, p. 582). But P. S. Minear, 'The Audience of the Fourth Evangelist,' *Interpretation* 31, 1977, pp. 344, 345 argues otherwise, suggesting a specific readership.

[3] There are other typically Johannine expressions in the 17th chapter: see Stephen S. Smalley, *John: Evangelist and Interpreter*, 1978, pp. 188–190.

[4] R. de Vaux, *The Early History of Israel*, vol. 1, 1978, pp. 455,456.

[5] R. Schnackenburg, *The Church in the New Testament*, E.T. 1965, pp. 103–113 for John's picture of the church; see too E. Schweizer, 'The Concept of the Church in the Gospel and Epistles of St. John,' *New Testament Essays: Studies in Memory of T. W. Manson*, ed. A. J. B. Higgins, 1959, pp. 230–245.

[6] The witness of the book of Revelation, especially in the letters

to the seven Asian churches (chs. 2,3) is germane here.

[7] E. Käsemann, *The Testament of Jesus*, ch. 4.

[8] B. A. Mastin, 'A Neglected Feature of the Christology of the Fourth Gospel,' *New Testament Studies*, 22, 1976, pp. 32–51, especially p. 46.

[9] R. E. Brown, 'The Kerygma of the Gospel according to John,' *Interpretation*, 21, 1967, pp. 397,398: 'The faith that John demands of the Christian . . . involves the acceptance of dogma, namely, the one basic christological dogma of the unity of Jesus with the Father. . . . John insists that faith, in order to be saving faith, must involve the affirmation that Jesus is the Son of God.'

[10] And 'unity' seems to require some kind of visible, though not necessarily organic, community, if 'we interpret xvii. 21–23 in the light of x. 16 with its stress on one sheep herd, one shepherd' (Brown, *John* vol. 2, p. 776, though he grants 'community' is more implicit than explicit in ch. 17). Questions of ecumenical relations are remote from this chapter, even if E. L. Wenger, ' "That They All May be One," ' *Expository Times*, 70, 1958–59, p. 333 tries to see here a basis for organic church unity. J. F. Randall, 'The Theme of Unity in John 17:20–23,' *Ephemerides Theologicae Lovaniensis*, 41, 1965, pp. 373–394, warns against using this prayer for unity out of John's context: 'He was writing much more in the perspective of keeping the Church one, than of making it one' (p. 394), so the problem of ecumenism was not the same then as it is now.

[11] J. Moltmann, *The Church in the Power of the Spirit*, 1977, p. 361. His italics.

Chapter Eight

[1] See J. A. Fitzmyer, 'Reconciliation in Pauline Theology' in *No Famine in the Land. Studies in Honor of John L. McKenzie*, edd. J. W. Flanagan and Anita W. Robinson, 1975, pp. 155,156 for nine ways Paul describes the new life in Christ.

[2] The appeal gains in relevance if 1 Peter is a document that incorporates sections of one or more baptismal sermons addressed to new converts who had recently professed the faith. See F. W. Beare, *The First Epistle of Peter*, third ed., 1970, pp. 216–226.

[3] See I. H. Marshall, *Kept by the Power of God*, 1969, ch. 6.

[4] See G. W. H. Lampe, 'Church Discipline and the Interpretation of the Epistles to the Corinthians', *Christian History and its Interpretation: Studies presented to John Knox*, edd. W. R. Farmer, C. F. D. Moule and R. R. Niebuhr, 1967, pp. 337–361, especially pp. 346–355. Repudiation of the faith in apostasy or by spreading a false christology which is other than that of Jesus as Son of God incarnate is the chief ground for excommunication in Lampe's judgment (p. 361).

[5] C. K. Barrett, *Paul's Second Epistle to the Corinthians*, p. 103.

[6] J. Murphy-O'Connor, *Paul on Preaching*, pp. 204, 205; cf. p.

259.

[7] Paul here is evidently drawing on a form of missionary preaching based on Jesus' lordship known in the church before he came along. See Paul-Emile Langevin, *Jésus Seigneur et l'eschatologie. Exégèse de textes prépauliniens*, 1967, pp. 43–106.

[8] The texts of patristic writers are considered by Dale Moody, 'The Origin of Infant Baptism,' in *The Teacher's Yoke. Studies in Memory of Henry Trantham*, edd. E. J. Vardaman and J. L. Garrett, 1964, pp. 189–202. Origen was the first to introduce the idea of baptism as cleansing away birth pollution, and Moody concludes: With the hammer of his theory of inherited guilt Augustine nailed down the lid that sealed this practice [of infant baptism] in the West until AD 1525, when the Anabaptists blew it off in Zollikon-Zurich (p. 201).

[9] 'It is not Communism that is condemned by the Bible: it is *totalitarianism*, a principle which may reign in capitalist countries just as well as in communist ones. . . . A state becomes totalitarian if it substitutes itself for God by "requesting worship," i.e. enslavement of consciences and the practice of morals overthrowing the divine laws (and above all, the practice of justice). Such a state has ceased to be a "minister of God," it has become a "minister of the Beast" [of Rev. 17]' (J. Héring, *A Good and a Bad Government According to the New Testament*, 1954, p. 43; his italics).

[10] R. Minnerath, *Les chrétiens et le monde*, 1973, pp. 332,333 uses these Corinthian verses to illustrate 'the paradox of the Christian' who faces 'the call to live *in* this world, without being *of* this world.'

The resolution of the paradox is in a relativizing of the values of the world by applying the criterion of living in the new order of salvation history – a world view derived from O. Cullmann's *Salvation in History*, E.T. 1967. 'The "as–if" of Paul is the key to the paradox of Christian existence set in this world' (p. 333), he concludes, appealing effectively to *Diognetus* 10.5–7 and 5.4–17.

Chapter Nine

[1] The church as a 'gathered community' can claim to represent a persistent theme in early Christian literature from the adverb in Acts 2:1: '*together* in one place' to Justin's description of worship at Rome in the mid-second century (*Apol.* 67). In *1 Clement* 34.7 the phrase is preceded by 'in accord.' Hermas' *9th Similitude* relates 'coming together' to 'becoming one body,' while Ignatius speaks of 'one prayer, one petition, one mind, one hope in love, in blameless joy' (*Magnesians* 7.1) and of the power of praying together to destroy Satan's influence (*Ephesians* 5.3, 13.1). J. Reiling ('Prophecy, the Spirit and the Church,' *Prophetic Vocation in the New Testament and Today*, pp. 60–66) cites also the contribution of the prophetic ministry when the church assembles as in Hebrews 10.25

(cf. *Barnabas* 4.10).

[2] See E. R. Goodenough, 'Symbolism, Jewish (in the Greco-Roman Period),' *Encyclopaedia Judaica*, vol. 15, 1971, pp. 568–578.

[3] Edwyn Bevan, *Holy Images*, 1940, pp. 113 dates the first appearance of the crucifix – a detached cross with a human figure on it – to the seventh century.

[4] This quotation and much of the evidence of what follows relating the Council's *De Sacra Liturgia* is taken from *Documents of Vatican II*, ed. A. P. Flannery, 1975, pp. 1–282.

[5] T. G. A. Baker, *Questioning Worship*, 1977, p. 11.

[6] Baker, p. 10. He regards the reforms as praiseworthy but still lacking in radical depth; and there is a debit side too: 'Aesthetic, emotional and spiritual impoverishment' follows in the wake of a loss of 'the sense of the numinous' and the modernity of language can offer instant communication at the expense of the language becoming banal, 'matey' and non-evocative of true worship directed to the mystery of God.

[7] Illustrated, for instance, in her title *Mater Ecclesiae* ('Mother of the Church') and depicted as such over the entrance to the Church of the Annunciation in Nazareth. The New Testament and second century witness to Mary's role is strikingly different, as the recent inter-confessional study, *Mary in the New Testament*, edd. R. E. Brown, K. P. Donfried, J. A. Fitzmyer and J. Reumann, 1978, has shown.

[8] Leon J. Cardinal Suenens, *A New Pentecost?* 1975, p. 210.

[9] J. M. Ford, *Six Pentecosts*, 1976, 'The Marian Pentecost,' pp. 7–14.

[10] George A. Maloney, 'Do Not Be Afraid to Take Mary Home,' *Catholic Charismatic*, 1, 4, 1976, pp. 32,33.

[11] Suenens, p. 207; Maloney, p. 33.

[12] This negative assessment is reinforced by reading Fr. Louis Pfaller and L. J. Alberts, *Mary Is Pentecostal*, 1973. See too *A Christian's Guide to Today's Catholic Charismatic Movement* compiled by James Neher, 1977.

[13] John V. Taylor, *The Go-Between God*, pp. 136f.

[14] See R. J. McKelvey, *The New Temple*, 1969.

Index of Principal Scriptures Discussed

Index of Subjects

Index of Modern Authors